W9-CIG-447

Ruin and Restitution

Ruin and Restitution

Reinterpreting Romanticism in Spain

❧

Philip W. Silver

Vanderbilt University Press

First printing 1997
97 98 99 00 4 3 2 1

This publication is made from recycled paper and meets the minimum requirements
of American National Standard for Information Sciences—Permanence of Paper for
Printed Library Materials ∞

Frontispiece: James Hanes, "The Model, the Artist, and Tradition," 1953.
Pen and brown ink, 19.5cm x 27 cm.

Library of Congress Cataloging-in-Publication Data

Silver, Philip W., 1932-
    Ruin and restitution : reinterpreting romanticism in Spain /
Philip W. Silver.
        p. cm.
    Includes bibliographical references and index.
    ISBN 0-8265-1289-5
    1. Romanticism—Spain. 2. Spanish literature—19th century—
History and criticism. 3. Spanish poetry—19th century-—History
and criticism. 4. Spanish poetry—20th century—History and
criticism. I. Title.
    PQ6071.S55 1997
    861'.509145--dc21   97-4823
                                                    CIP

Manufactured in the United States of America

to my wife, Cristina Vizcaino Auger

It is as a political force that the aesthetic still concerns us as one of the most powerful ideological
drives to act upon the reality of history.

—Paul de Man, *The Rhetoric of Romanticism*

A historical people *are* through the dialogue
between their own and other languages.

—Martin Heidegger, *Hölderlins Hymne 'Der Ister'*

CONTENTS

PREFACE

This work is not primarily a history of Spanish romanticism nor a study of select Spanish romantic writers. Its goal is more fundamental. Since I take present perceptions of romanticism in Spain to be largely flawed, my purpose here is, first, to depose the present paradigm—if it can be called that—and second, to replace it with a different paradigm. In the process I hope to prepare for a richer understanding of Spanish postromantic poetry, the origins of which are at present unproductively entangled with Latin American *modernismo*. The position I advance in this regard is that although a hiatus between so-called Spanish romanticism and modern Spanish poetry does exist it can no longer be papered over with vague references to Bécquer and Rosalía de Castro, nor to Rubén Darío and José Martí.

The first time I approached this complex of problems was in response to an invitation by Francisco Rico to a course at the Menéndez y Pelayo Summer University in Santander. I am much obliged to him because it was there that I presented for the first time what I now call a restitutive solution to these problems. I also want to thank Professors Lasagabaster and Ascunce of the Universidad de Deusto (Mundaiz) in San Sebastián, who invited me to work with them on Spanish Romanticism and thus benefit from a grant from the Spanish Ministry of Education and Science. I am grateful for their encouragement, even though I finally finished *Ruin and Restitution* while on a generous Fulbright Senior Scholar Fellowship in 1995–1996.

Because this book has taken so long to complete, the list of people whose help I should like to acknowledge has grown outsize. But for their early encouragement I want first to pay a debt of gratitude to my former professors at Princeton University, Vicente Llorens, Edmund L. King, and Claudio Guillén. Then, for their wisdom and material help, I want to thank my colleagues at Columbia University, especially Félix Martínez Bonati, Patricia Grieve, Gonzalo Sobejano, Alfred MacAdam, Herbert Klein, and Edward Malefakis, and also my editor at Vanderbilt University Press, Bard Young. I am also grateful to fellow scholars Inman Fox, Joan Ramón Resina, Manuel Ballbé, Robert Marrast, Mikel Azurmendi, Guillermo Carnero, David T. Gies, Randolph Pope, Brian Dendle, Donald L. Shaw, Derek Flitter, Christopher Maurer, Jacobo Cortines, Rafael Montesinos, William Sherzer, Juan Casamayor, María Angeles Naval, and Peter Silver, and to the students in my Romanticism seminars. And for their help and friendship I thank Saúl Yurkievich, José María San Sebastián, Claudio Rodríguez, Clara Miranda, Antonio García Berrio, Javier Muguerza, and the editors and *contertulios* of the journal *Bitarte* in San Sebastián.

Philip W. Silver

INTRODUCTION

Romanticism and Postromantic Poetry

The verse "We are all romantics. . . . Who is there that is not?" by the Nicaraguan poet Rubén Darío, correctly signals a lack of clarity about Romanticism in Hispanic letters.[1] Although Darío was writing in 1907, a similar uncertainty persists today among Hispanists. Opinion is divided, and although most scholars speak as though there were a Spanish Romanticism, there is no consensus about just where, between 1794 and 1898, to locate it.

My invocation of Rubén Darío is doubly rhetorical. He was such a strong Latin American poet that he was praised by late nineteenth-century Spanish critics for reawakening Peninsular poetry. But those of us who are literary historians ought to wonder at this personification of such a vital segment of Spanish literary history in the figure of Rubén Darío and ask, What would we do if he had never existed? For the feat he allegedly accomplished for modern Spanish poetry, and that he is said to embody—no less than its aggiornamento; he was, after all, a "modernista"—is what Spanish literary history presently has instead of an understanding of its romanticism. In the essay that follows I offer a new approach to the understanding of romanticism in Spain—more as a lack than as a precursor.

Ruin and Restitution[2] resulted from questions that arose in studying twentieth-century Spanish poetry. Compared with its French, German, and English counterparts, why does the progress of nineteenth- and twentieth-century Spanish poetry seem so halting and curiously foreshortened? For example, Baroque poetry by Góngora reappears for a time in the poetry of the "Generation of 1927," perhaps because so little first-rate poetry has intervened. There is also the literary "belatedness" of Spain vis-à-vis Europe since 1700. In contrast to its inventiveness and literary imperialism—the picaresque novel, Don Juan and Don Quixote, the influence of Spanish mysticism on English Metaphysicals—Spain, in the eighteenth and nineteenth centuries, only seems prodigal in late European imitations. This was why Mesonero Romanos spoke of his country as "una nación traducida" ("a translated nation"). No longer ahead, or even à la page, from 1700 to 1828, Spanish literature seems to have survived by recycling its literary past. And, in view of the critical assumption that all modern poetry is a direct or indirect heir of romanticism, twentieth-century Spanish scholars have attributed nineteenth-century poetry's lack of distinction to a weak Enlightenment and a diffident romantic movement.[3] In this view, a deficient Spanish romanticism could produce only pusillanimous poetic offspring. This seems a fair description of late nineteenth-century poetry, graced only, following its brief romantic "heyday," by Bécquer's Rimas of 1871 and Rosalía de Castro's En las orillas del Sar[4] of 1884.

The trouble with this picture is that, with the publication of Juan Ramón Jiménez's Arias tristes and Antonio Machado's Soledades in 1903, Spanish poetry begins making up for lost time. If it is no exaggeration to speak of twentieth-century Spanish poetry as a second Golden Age, this is because with Unamuno, Valle-Inclán, Juan Ramón Jiménez, the two Machados, García Lorca, Jorge Guillén, Pedro Salinas, Luis Cernuda, Rafael Alberti, Dámaso Alonso, Miguel Hernández, Gerardo Diego, Leopoldo Panero, Luis Rosales, Blas de Otero, Gabriel Celaya, Gloria Fuertes, Jaime Gil de Biedma, Angel González, Francisco Brines, Julia Uceda, José Angel Valente, Claudio Rodríguez, Guillermo Carnero, Ana Rossetti, and Antonio Colinas, Castilian poetry overtakes European poetry and ceases to be belated. The sudden preeminence of modern Spanish poetry must mean that Spain is a counterexample to the belief that relates national romanticism to modern poetry as cause to effect, since, without a strong precursor romanticism, Spain's twentieth-century poetry is second to none. This phenomenon suggests that either the real status of its national romanticism is misunderstood in the case of Spain, or that Spain is not as bereft of romanticism as has been supposed.

Therefore, nothing will enhance our understanding of postromantic Spanish poetry as much as a reexamination of Spanish romanticism. At present the literary and historical relations between European and Spanish romanticism, and of both with modern Spanish poetry, are misconstrued. The first step in expounding the essential discontinuity between Spanish romanticism and modern Spanish poetry is to show that early views of Spanish romanticism were highly ideological.[5] Because debates about romanticism always have long histories, it behooves us to take seriously the political aspects of these, whether Spanish or European. For even if literary romanticism was not strong in Spain, the heated discussions surrounding it suggest that it played a significant role in the struggle of the bourgeoisie to establish an economically and politically unified nation-state. For this reason the problem of Spanish romanticism is best approached in the context of this bourgeois struggle for hegemony. Indeed, if modern critics have failed to find a Spanish romanticism to their liking, it is probably because the only romanticism there, and which Spanish liberalism could tolerate, was a conservative romanticism, in step with the *moderado* mentality of the time. Members of the "Generation of 1898," and later Republican critics, were so appalled by the Restoration's governance of Spain, that they imagined a liberal political and literary romanticism that had not in fact been there. They failed to credit the interrelatedness of historical Romanticism, their own bourgeois revolution, and the romantic historiography written between 1840 and 1870, when politician-historians formed our present view of much medieval and modern Spanish history. This was despite the fact that a historically oriented romantic theater, historical novels in imitation of Scott, the romantic historiography, and historical-ballad collections, as well as elite reworkings of folktale and folk song, made up a substantial, politically interested, albeit conservative, romanticism. Finally, exiled Republican scholars misread the romantic posturings of Espronceda and Larra and treated them as though they were European-style high romantics. Even though the quintessential Spanish romantic poet, Gustavo Adolfo Bécquer (1836–1870), had always exhibited a late conservative, Catholic, medievalizing variety of romanticism. In fact, as our examination of Bécquer's prose and poetry will show, the notion of European high romanticism fits Spanish, that is, Castilian-Andalusian, romanticism not at all.[6]

However, romanticism is an international and not only a national event; it must therefore be pursued across national and disciplinary borders. So to take the measure of European high romanticism and prepare for the critical examination of Bécquer's and Cernuda's work, in addition to examining the existing theories of Spanish romanticism, I also review Paul de Man's critique of Anglo-American romantic studies. This has its origins in what he called "historical poetics," an extrapolation of

Hölderlin's poetic theory with which he first sought to contest postromantic literary history. By bringing to bear this "historical poetics"—in
the context of Heidegger's concept of "resolute repetition"—it becomes
possible to compare the "ruined" state of Spanish romanticism with Paul
de Man's deconstruction of European high romanticism.

Besides altering perceptions of the relation between romanticism
and modern poetry, since Spanish literary history has proved misleading,
I also propose replacing our present belief in literary teleology with a version of Heidegger's "resolute repetition." This would enable the description of a counterhistorical tradition, more in keeping with the
Longinian-Kantian notion of poetic genius. To illustrate this antitradition, *Ruin and Restitution* also focuses on the poetry of Luis Cernuda
(1902– 1963) as a *contemporary* "romantic" poet whose work demonstrates how Spanish "postromantic" poets have built their work from the
detritus of European high romanticism, thereby providing Spain with a
sui generis restitution of the same.

Obviously we traverse an uneven literary, historical, and political
terrain. Virtually no term used here goes uncontested today. At the same
time, it is striking that the nearer we draw to the central insights afford-
ed by high romanticism, the less aberrant a self-conscious or "destructive" critical enterprise appears. After all, it is precisely the work of those
literary critics and comparatists, whose understanding of romanticism
seems most profound, that recently confronted us with a radical revision
of literary studies. In the main, these comparatists exposed the "infelici-
ties" of the terms on which we would still like to depend. Especially Paul
de Man and others of the "Yale School" rendered controversial such
terms as *romanticism, literature, literary history* and even *history*. In fact,
there seems to be a reverse correlation between sensitivity to a certain
reading of the insights of high romanticism and acclaim of the New
History, even now being brushed aside by Cultural Studies.

I make no apology for the speculative nature of this enterprise. The
proposition that there could be a literary history, a literary criticism, or
even a historiography beyond the reach of philosophy and literary theory
can only be advanced as a defensive strategy. But the ahistorical prioritiz-
ing of theory cannot be allowed to pass either. It is not beside the point
that European comparatists of philosophical orientation still constitute
one vanguard of romantic studies.[7] While this would seem to confirm our

academic fascination with the exotic, it also may reveal something about romanticism. What is there about this movement that so energized exiled and other literary critics? Perhaps it is its unspoken, if not always unspeakable, national undertones—which are not negligible in the case of Spain. Or perhaps the early European romantics were as concerned as contemporary critics with the philosophical nature of writing.[8] At least we have the *Frühromantik* of Jena to thank for declaring that modern poetry must be *romantic*, which is the name of our confusion and the point of departure for the present book.

Is the result of my study the depiction of a "Spanish high romantic movement" that we can point to as precursor of a modern poetry? Only in the special restitutional sense described below. In any case I believe that the discussion achieves a gain in clarity because my scrutiny of romanticism will show: first, that a conservative-liberal romanticism helped a nationalistic political centralism consolidate a factitiously unitary Spanish culture; second, that Spain produced no high romantic *movement* per se; third, that the *discontinuity* romanticism–contemporary poetry is compensated for by a *piecemeal restitution of high romanticism*; fourth, that this redefinition of Spanish romanticism will provide new understanding of many other poets besides Bécquer and Cernuda; and last, that a literary movement like romanticism, that evades all attempts to contain it, still has much to teach us. This is why, instead of writing a history of Spanish romanticism, I opted for the present Foucaultian genealogical approach. In part as a hedge against the possibility that in failing to write a historical account of the discontinuum romantic-postromantic Castilian-Andalusian poetry, I have only accumulated notes for its antithesis: an ontology of poetry.

Finally, a word of explanation about the frontispiece. In this circumstance James Hanes's pen and ink drawing allegorizes "historical poetics" and thus, indirectly, Spain's too-mimetic reading of romanticism. The historical consequence is that the artist's model virtually escapes stylization while the artist himself is diminished, because he failed to view his subject in terms of the (ruined) tradition that surrounds them both.

Ruin and Restitution

CHAPTER I

$\mathcal{R}$omanticism and the
$\mathcal{I}$nvention of $\mathcal{M}$odern $\mathcal{S}$pain

It has long been supposed that a liberal romanticism appeared in Spain following the death of Fernando VII. But as early as the Trienio Liberal (1820–1823) Spanish liberalism had begun to splinter, and a powerful liberal-conservative amalgam of interests emerged after 1833. This sociopolitical entente dictated that literary romanticism in Spain would be essentially conservative. Reciprocally, this romanticism was drafted into casting the bourgeois revolution in a positive light. Although Spanish romanticism's historical retro-vision served to enhance a developing authoritarian liberalism, the resulting alienation of Spanish history from a national project increased late nineteenth-century pessimism at the liberal failure to consolidate a unified, nonauthoritarian nation-state. In this chapter I argue that although political circumstances worked against even conservative literary romanticism ever becoming a coherent literary movement, it was nevertheless disseminated as a nationalistic politico-literary ideology throughout the nineteenth century. Section 1 gives the reasons for this conservatism in Spanish liberalism and romanticism. In section 2 I suggest a correspondence between moderate liberal political praxis and the largely eighteenth-century aesthetics of Spanish romanticism. Section 3 examines the nationalism-centralism in mid-century bourgeois historiography as "romantic nationalism." The thrust of section 4 is an interpretation of the "neoromanticism" of the Generation of 1898 as the centralist response to late nineteenth-century micro-nationalism. And Section 5 intimates that Spain's late and explosive proletarian revolution and its present national separatist difficulties are also consequences of Spain's unregenerate authoritarian liberalism.

Historical Romanticism as Moderate Liberal Ideology[1]

❧ We begin with this paradox: although there is no clear consensus among specialists as to the very existence of a Spanish romanticism, ever since the end of the late eighteenth century Spain has been considered a romantic country. To add to the confusion, scholars have lately drawn attention to the strong reaction among Spanish authors, themselves romantics *against* French-inspired liberal romanticism.[2] This suggests that Spain does not know how romantic it is. The problem is partly that instead of conceptualizing a romanticism of their own, Spaniards had the label thrust upon them. This misunderstanding began because the Schlegel brothers found Spain's cultural mixture of medieval and Golden Age so very "romantic." This has served to excuse Spaniards, as Aullón de Haro ironically points out, from ever having to distinguish between romantic doctrine and historical truth.[3] Indeed, subsequent criticism of Spanish romanticism has done little to reduce this lack of precision.

As Aullón de Haro observes, it is clear that Spaniards were not romantics *avant la lettre*, to judge by their resistance to the Schlegels' ideas when Böhl de Faber, a foreign consul in Cádiz, expounded them in 1814–1819.[4] At least, José Joaquín de Mora, who publicly responded to Böhl de Faber, was a patriotic *afrancesado* with liberal Enlightenment convictions. His polemic with Böhl showed that Spain was not ready for even a conservative romanticism. When Böhl de Faber, closely following A. W. Schlegel's *Vorlesungen über dramatische Kunst und Literatur* (1809–1811), suggested that Christianity, romantic or modern art, and political conservatism belonged together, J. Joaquín de Mora objected angrily if anonymously.

Indeed, liberal critics ever since have resisted the notion that Spanish Romanticism could be anything but liberal. Until recently this involved denying the importance of Böhl de Faber as promoter of the first conservative romantic ideas in Spain. Misled by their liberal parti pris, critics were reluctant to acknowledge that in applying Schlegel's version of Herder's ideas, Böhl de Faber drew the outline of what was to be the dominant romanticism in Spain: one that was politically conservative, Catholic, and that focused on the reform and revitalization of national values.[5] That it was conservative in precisely this way guaranteed that it would harmonize with the predominantly *moderado* cast of

Spanish liberalism.[6] Given this contradictory beginning, it is no surprise that little progress has been made toward a consensus about Spanish romanticism. On the Liberal-Republican side, the conviction has been that romanticism was introduced into Spain by returning liberal exiles after the death of Fernando VII in 1833. Once the rancor surrounding the Spanish Civil War (1936–1939) receded, partisans of the conservative Böhl de Faber's importance, like Hans Juretschke, began to draw attention to other nineteenth-century theorists of conservative romanticism such as Agustín Durán and Alberto Lista. But the response by those favoring a liberal romanticism was to insist that no romanticism, conservative or otherwise, had existed in Spain prior to 1833; and to assert that throughout the "ominosa década" (1823–1833) a *genuine* Spanish romanticism existed only among liberal exiles abroad.

But there has also been a problem with defining romanticism itself. Contemporary liberal critics such as Vicente Llorens, R. Navas-Ruiz, and Iris Zavala, provide masses of historical content but fudge their basic definition of romanticism, whether international or local.[7] By and large these partisans of liberal romanticism take Larra (1809–1837) and Espronceda (1808–1842) as prototypes, and center their definition on cosmic protest and metaphysical anguish.[8] Richard Cardwell, for example, put in circulation a notion of Spanish romanticism as proto-existentialism.[9] In an article on the Generation of 1927, he suggested that the Spanish Romantics were anguished precursors of the 1927 generation of poets, because "the literary scene in the 1920s had strong affinities with that of the 1830s and 1840s." In this reading, Larra, Espronceda, Azorín, and Rafael Alberti all suffered a similar metaphysical crisis. Curiously, Cardwell's 1970 essay is also taken as retroactive confirmation of the existence of a Spanish *high* romanticism.[10]

In constructing a more sophisticated albeit still European model for Spanish liberal romanticism, Susan Kirkpatrick opined that "Spanish Romanticism . . . developed models of the lyric subject that bore close resemblance to their counterparts in the rest of Europe, and that were, like them, distinctly gender-specific."[11] But her argument is based partly on a misconstrual of sentences from Larra's 1836 article, "Literature." Professor Kirkpatrick is convinced that Larra connects his "Liberal revolutionary program" to the "literary agenda of Romanticism" because she believes his references in this essay to "passions" and "imagination" are genuine indices of romanticism.[12] Yet it is just as likely that Larra is recalling Hugh Blair's much translated *Lectures on Rhetoric and Belles Lettres* of 1783, which is hardly a romantic text. At any rate, because Larra, her romantic icon, is far from typical in his insights, his case does not favor generalization.

Even the best critics, like Susan Kirkpatrick, at least implicitly impute a European-style high romanticism to Spain. That is, they employ a definition of *high* romanticism in accord with specialists of English and European romanticism such as René Wellek and Meyer H. Abrams. But because the core of this definition is "the possible-impossible expansion of the self to a seamless identification with the universe," it overshoots any Spanish mark I am aware of.[13]

In fact, if we interrogate the history, literature, and politics of the heyday of Spanish romanticism (1834–1844), we find no liberal high romantic movement; indeed, a "European-style" high romanticism is nowhere to be seen. Two outstanding liberal romantics—Larra and Espronceda—do not by themselves make a movement, and it is by no means certain that either was a high romantic. Although by most accounts Espronceda was extremely liberal, like Larra his work reveals the deep imprint of an Enlightenment education. What is more, after Larra's suicide in 1837, when José de Zorrilla became suddenly famous, a strong reaction against the very idea of a too liberal romanticism ensued. Indeed, Robert Marrast sees Mesonero Romanos, who launched the popular *Semanario Pintoresco*, as the spokesperson for a decidedly reactionary bourgeois "national-romanticism."[14]

Fortunately, a new benchmark is available against which to measure definitions of Spanish romanticism. Using Morse Peckham's aperçu regarding two discrete chronological phases of European romanticism—the first releasing radical tensions, the second seeking an accommodation—Virgil Nemoianu characterizes the second of these as Biedermeier romanticism. If Abramsian high romanticism, the first phase, is the secularization of a Christian plot, then Biedermeier, according to Nemoianu, is a further secularization of that plot. It is instructive to use Nemoianu's parameters for Biedermeier in order to tidy up a heretofore ill-defined Spanish romanticism. For instance, some of the characteristics of "national-romanticism" that Marrast lists in his study of Espronceda—"aburguesamiento," the refurbishing of Enlightenment ideals, "bourgeois" nationalism, and an idiosyncratic individualism—are also Biedermeier traits, as is the sentimental Catholic romanticism of Böhl de Faber's novelist daughter, Fernán Caballero. In fact Nemoianu calls Fernan Caballero's *costumbrismo* "the most significant manifestation of the Spanish Biedermeier."[15] Finally, the second, Biedermeier, phase can even appear where there was no *native* high romanticism; in other words, Biedermeier can be seen as the "taming [of] an absent romanticism."

Biedermeier could also be useful in the specific case of the relationship between Espronceda and romanticism. For despite the common perception, Espronceda was not truly an Abramsian high romantic, either in his *Canciones*, *El Estudiante de Salamanca* or in *El diablo mundo*. In adapting Byron's ironic discourse to the Spanish milieu, Espronceda merely called attention to his own belatedness, as he did by his sympathy for Heine's ridicule of the *Frühromantik*. Thus, a case could also be made for Espronceda's poetry as Biedermeier-ish. After all, he was the exact contemporary of the 1830 libertarian, but still Catholic, French romantics known as "petits romantiques." Still, while Biedermeier might help to reformulate features of a late post-1844 Spanish "national-romanticism," there are points that tell against its systematic employ as a general characterization of all Spanish romanticism. While it can account for the pale mid-century romanticism of Fernán Caballero, it ill accommodates the kitsch medievalism of the earlier conservative romanticism that Hans Juretschke labeled "historical Romanticism," Derek Flitter "Romantic historicism," and Robert Marrast "traditional or national-romanticism." Nor can it entirely account for Spain's strong negative reaction to French liberal romanticism or for the bourgeoisie's obsession with a simulacrum of its nation's medieval past.[16]

Why, then, is Spanish literary romanticism such a difficult nut to crack? Partly this is because of its incompletely acknowledged sociopolitical entailments. Partisans of a liberal romanticism have not entirely ignored this aspect. Yet when we scrutinize Spanish history between the death of Fernando VII and 1844, there is little sign of the liberal romanticism its partisans lead us to expect. On the contrary, the true message of this historical period—the decade from 1834 to 1844—is that romanticism was immersed, almost to the point of inanition, in the bourgeois struggle for political and ideological hegemony. Noteworthy, however, is the fact that the genesis of a *native* conservative literary romanticism and of what historians call the liberal revolutionary cycle occupy the same years—from 1808 until 1843. Thus, when Bécquer's friend and mentor, González Bravo, became Prime Minister in 1843, this marked the end of the "revolutionary" cycle, as R. L. Blanco Valdés says, but also the beginning of *moderado hegemony* and of "the incremental construction of a centralized, militarized, oligarchic State, impervious to democratic reform."[17]

Therefore, instead of the alleged "liberal romanticism," the dominant romanticism was conservative, a perfect reflection of what was in fact a liberal-conservative pact between an anemic bourgeoisie and a still powerful nobility. Because this pact was illiberal in the extreme, it required a convincing justification, and the best one available was the conservative romanticism that soon won ascendancy. Therefore, to fathom *literary* romanticism in Spain we must scrutinize the actual bourgeois struggle to consolidate a unified nation-state. For although the coincidence of nation building with political and literary romanticism was by no means unique to Spain, the atypical demise of its ancien régime certainly was. Instead of being swept away, supporters of the old régime were able to dictate their own terms.

This was possible in part because the Enlightenment in Spain failed to revolutionize agricultural technology, which in turn delayed the industrialization of other sectors of the economy. In addition, Spain in the early nineteenth century also lacked a unified national market and then began to lose its colonial markets as well. This meant that Spanish capitalism was forced into a dependency on the capitalism of other, more advanced European countries.[18] These and other factors kept the ancien régime itself from developing an adequate framework for a capitalist economy. But the principal reason for the failure of Spanish liberalism was the weakness and dispersion of Spain's urban bourgeoisie, who were incapable of directing the revolutionary process. However, this situation was perfectly natural, given the "economic, political, and cultural relations of dominance" that had pertained under the ancien régime. According to Antonio Elorza, without a national market the bourgeoisie's weakness was guaranteed, which in turn forced it to seek strong allies among the nobility, given the bourgeoisie's incapacity to construct a "liberal Spain" by itself.[19]

Some of these revelations about Spanish liberalism have surfaced in the debate about the degree to which any social transformation at all took place under the ancien régime. Ever since Miguel Artola's *Los orígenes de la España contemporánea* (1954), most research has supported his contention that beginning in 1760–1765, modernization, including economic and social change, did work structural changes that prepared the way for capitalism and a liberal bourgeois revolution.[20]

At the same time, as Antonio-Miguel Bernal says, since in Spain the Enlightenment had much *less* impact on social change, a genuine break with the ancien régime was possible only

> after hard, slow and difficult negotiations, as the result of a *pacted solution* that primarily entailed the insertion of the Ancien Régime, with its political—somewhat reduced—economic and social connotations into the new liberal and bourgeois order, at least for several decades after the latter had been established by law.[21]

This suggests the precariousness of the hegemony of the Spanish bourgeoisie as compared with the control wielded by sectors of the ancien régime.[22] These reactionary sectors managed to control the political groups that ruled post-1833 governments. This was possible because their base was in agriculture, the leading sector of the economy throughout the nineteenth century. Indeed, given their powerful leverage, the nobility was able,

> by means of the process of ecclesiastical and civil disentailment and because of the manner in which it was carried out—the termination of the seigneurial régime—to maintain and even improve on the advantageous economic position they had enjoyed under the feudal class system.[23]

Thus, according to Josep Fontana, what was peculiar about the transformation of society in Spain was the nobility's virtual control of the transition to capitalism, on their own terms and for their own benefit.[24]

Of course, this deep mutual implication of Spanish politics and romanticism has been remarked by literary critics and historians before. However, the inference usually drawn is that while a genuine liberalism and a liberal romanticism worked in harmony, the opposition of a countervailing Spanish traditionalism justified the shortcomings of both. For example, Susan Kirkpatrick argues that liberal romanticism helped install the bourgeois values of nationalism, freedom, and individual subjectivity and, hence, that Spanish romanticism provided liberalism with its ideology. At the same time, she also recognizes that the implantation of liberal values was superficial due to the opposition of reactionary political and cultural forces.

With the shortcomings of liberalism and romanticism thus explained, she is free to treat Larra and Espronceda as though they were European-style high romantics; at the same time she acknowledges that liberal political reforms in Spain were truncated and that liberal romanticism was not necessarily dominant. Despite the panache of her argument, it would be stronger if she distanced Spanish romanticism from liberalism and recognized that both conservatives and liberals were in competition to promote a common conservative nationalistic Romanticism. Indeed, it is difficult to understand the general reluctance to acknowledge—as Kirkpatrick ultimately does—that the *majority* romanticism was *essentially* conservative and indeed a faithful reflection of an involutionary 1812 liberalism. As Spanish liberalism grew progressively conservative, even during the Trienio Liberal, the only literary romanticism with any chance of success became a backward-looking historical Romanticism.

In contrast to the literary critics' focus on romantic individualism, the Catalán historian J. Vicens Vives has proposed a societal approach. He characterizes the period from 1780 to 1830 as one of economic optimism, expansion, and demographic growth. For Vicens Vives the distinctive feature of this era is not romantic angst but romantic reformism. The spread of this "diffuse feeling in favor of social reform," which affected revolutionaries and counterrevolutionaries alike, was of greater moment than even the French Revolution.[25] Of course, romantic reformism assumed a different valence in either case. When romanticism was combined with liberal reformism the emphasis fell on freedom and the political self, which scarcely happened in Spain. But when romanticism was combined with traditionalist reformism the result was a conservative ideology. As Vicens Vives explains, traditionalist reformism, "forced to legitimize a cause it no longer could nor should justify in terms of the ancien régime, found 'legitimate' support for its plan and its acts by resurrecting a supposedly admirable Medieval way of life."[26]

Thus a kitsch medievalism—"archaic, gothic, chivalric, feudal"—became, in conservative romantic hands, what Vicens Vives has called a *strategy of legitimation*. In other words, it served to disguise reactionary longings for literary, social, and political reform. But then the same medieval-idyll strategy that had served as a conservative historical legitimation attracted the liberals as well. And thus the aesthetic interests of conservatism and liberalism converged, to their mutual benefit and to the detriment of the "canalla" (or rabble, as the serf-like masses were called).[27] In short, a previously existing conservative national historical Romanticism was extended to facilitate shared conservative-liberal bourgeois, that is *moderado*, political interests. For in truth the best-kept secret of nineteenth-century Spanish liberalism was the existential insecurity of its adherents as a class. As Gil Novales remarks of Spain's shaky bourgeois revolution, "A bourgeois transformation, yes, but always accompanied by an extraordinary fear, first of the French Revolution, and later of Socialism."[28] This is why Nemoianu's notion of a tamed Biedermeier romanticism dovetails so neatly with the *moderado* mentality of the Spanish romantics, including Espronceda and Larra.

Thus far I have spoken variously of a liberal and a conservative romanticism, of a national-romanticism (Marrast), a historical Romanticism (Juretschke), a Romantic historicism (Flitter), and a Biedermeier romanticism (Nemoianu). The time has come to introduce a measure of terminological order. Although Marrast's, Juretschke's, or Flitter's terms would serve to designate what I view as the majority conservative-liberal romanticism, Juretschke's seems the most promising term to date. At the same time, Marrast's "national-romanticism" also captures the fundamental *retrospective* "romantic national" component that I believe is crucial *within* Juretschke's historical Romanticism.[29] For this reason I shall henceforth choose Juretschke's historical Romanticism for what I have been referring to as a conservative-liberal, and also *moderado*, literary romanticism. Juretschke's term will henceforth apply to the period from roughly 1814 to 1844. And I will reserve Marrast's national-romanticism, together with Nemoianu's Biedermeier, for the later post-1844 hegemonic period of *moderantismo*—which lasts at least to 1868. I find this term of Marrast's especially apt for extreme cases of "romantic nationalism" such as Mesonero Romanos and Zorrilla. I am guided, in making this allocation of terms, by the conviction that what Jover Zamora has called "romantic nationalism," and which originated *within* the prevailing historical Romanticism, is also present in romantic historians like Modesto Lafuente, and later in Bécquer, as well as in outstanding members of the Generation of 1898.[30] Hence, my use of Marrast's national-romanticism and Biedermeier to refer to these later, post–historical romantic manifestations of "romantic nationalism."

Derek Flitter's carefully reasoned use of "Romantic historicism" as an inclusive designation merits a discussion apart. The contention of his *Spanish Romantic Literary Theory and Criticism* (1992) is that "the principles of Romantic historicism, stemming from the work of Herder and more fully expounded with reference to literary history by the Schlegel brothers, . . . dominated Spanish literary theory during the whole of the period under discussion" (his study covers 1804–1850).[31] In practice, however, Flitter's contention amounts to a strong, new thesis about the consistency of a (conservative) Spanish romantic movement. For Flitter the very coherence of (this) Spanish romanticism lies in the gradual adoption by both conservatives *and liberals*—theorists such as López Soler, Durán, and Lista, but also Larra—of Böhl de Faber's rendering of A. W. Schlegel's and Herder's ideas.

But it seems to me that Flitter's strong thesis is weakened by the fact that its Herderian core of historicism tends to dissipate *conceptually* in the surrounding "historical Romanticism" of which Juretschke speaks, as it seems to have done in the actual historical world of 1834–1850. Both its terminological and its historical permeability, at least, make Flitter's "Romantic historicism" less satisfactory as a defining concept. That the entity to which Juretschke's "historical Romanticism" refers amounted to a full-fledged, self-conscious *literary movement* is, of course, just as unlikely. If there is a problem with Juretschke's term, it is not that its referent lacked critical mass, as is the case with "liberal romanticism." On the contrary, historical Romanticism was both more and less than a literary *movement*. For example, the only occasions when historical Romantics were moved to define themselves—with references to a "good romanticism"—was in reaction to French romanticism, which they perceived in the 1830s as politically and literarily threatening. Thus, Lista and other newly convinced historical Romantics only acknowledged their historical Romanticism as the lesser, because homegrown, evil. In this sense, Juretschke's historical Romanticism designates less a normal literary movement than an increasingly widespread *community of thought*, professed by an ever larger *moderado* sector of liberalism.

In other words, historical Romanticism, that is to say, the prevailing conservative-liberal romanticism, was protean—a current of opinion, a strategy of legitimation, a general ambience—rather than a strictly literary happening. To have acknowledged that historical Romanticism was anything more would have drawn attention to the underlying reasons for its patent romantic nationalism—the way, for instance, romantic nationalism was used as prophylaxis against the different enemies of conservative-liberalism: such as the Carlists, the Progressives, the *populacho*, popular revolution, as well as genuine traditionalism. In this way *moderado* Spain of the "liberal" 1834–1844 decade embraced a historical Romanticism: (1) that was of the heart, of feeling and sentiment; (2) that involved the gradual loosening of neoclassical rules; (3) that was retrospective, patriotic, and ultimately ahistorical—although capable of discovering romantic nationalism even in Golden Age drama; and (4) that carried within it a peculiar catachresis of Herderian Romantic historicism as animating principle. Not simply Herder's or the Schlegels' literary historical idea that literature must reflect its era and nation, but historicism as an ideological message of bogusly retrospective, essentialist, bourgeois romantic nationalism.[32] Indeed, the original romantic nationalism that first appeared within historical Romanticism was not one content among others, but the *form* that held the thematics of historical Romanticism together. In this way, without having a clearly defined romantic *movement*, Spain became a "romantic" country despite itself. And since Spanish romanticism exercised this largely mediating role, it became for later critics a will-o'-the-wisp: historical Romanticism was everywhere and nowhere. And Spain became its own romantic parody.

"Moderado" Aesthetics and Politics: Lista and Espronceda

En política, por ejemplo, se llamó a lo antiguo *despotismo*, y a lo nuevo *libertad*; y tan indeterminantes, tan oscuros eran estos nombres como los de *clasicismo* y *romanticismo* adoptados para significar lo antiguo y lo nuevo en literatura . . . si los hechos eran oscuros ¿cómo no lo habían de ser los nombres, que son las fórmulas de los hechos?
—Gabino Tejado, "Poesía dramática," *El Laberinto*, 2 (1845), 202.[33]

Now, with historical Romanticism redefined, and a version of romantic nationalism identified as its ideological core and force, we must exemplify its unexpectedly eighteenth-century aesthetic and political shadings and illustrate their transmission from Alberto Lista (1775–1848) to his pupils, especially José de Espronceda (1808–1842). Bear in mind that for Lista aesthetics and politics were not separate undertakings and that this same mixture is palpable in the life and works of Espronceda. Here I employ Lista, an important second generation *reformista ilustrado*, and Espronceda, one of two emblematic Spanish romantic poets, to illustrate the consanguinity of *moderado* aesthetics and politics and to underline the heterogeneous, even haphazard, make-up of historical Romanticism as romanticism.

If, as Virgil Nemoianu holds, first phase, European high romanticism was an abrupt fruition of the social and cultural "implications and potentialities" of a "large human model," gradually formed during the eighteenth century, then a consonant *pre*romanticism would be these same potentialities in isolation *before* they coalesced in a high romanticism.[34] Such a preromanticism would be a more precise image of what is mistakenly perceived now as Spanish high romanticism. In Spain, and hence the illustrative value of Espronceda's case, although isolated ingredients of a *possible* high and low romanticism appeared, they failed to instantiate a *high* romanticism since they lacked what Nemoianu terms "the support of an integrated model."

At the Colegio de San Mateo in Madrid, between 1821 and 1825, together with Gómez Hermosilla, Alberto Lista instructed some of the best of the romantic generation of 1830, among them Espronceda. But the purpose of Lista's private school—as opposed to Quintana's attempts to reform public education—was to prepare elite *moderado* leaders, or what Gramsci called "organic intellectuals." For Lista and Gómez Hermosilla were also important architects of the political rationale of the *moderado* position, as well as integral parts of the social projection of what Antonio Elorza calls "authoritarian liberalism." Their teaching and writing was basic to the *moderado* effort to convert the society of the ancien régime into an adequate liberal framework for the development of capitalism.[35] Therefore, they are excellent examples of Vicens Vives's romantic reformism that inspired so many conservative-liberal politicians.

Indeed, Alberto Lista's political essays span almost the entire liberal revolutionary cycle, appearing first in *El Espectador Sevillano* (1809–1810), then during the Trienio Liberal (1820–1823) in *El Censor* and *El Imparcial*, and, during the "ominosa década," in the *Gaceta de Bayona* (1828–1830) and the *Estafeta de San Sebastián* (1830–1831).[36] Over these twenty-two years, Lista's early views were so altered by the revolutionary fervor of the Trienio Liberal that he eventually reacted to the July 1830 Revolution by rejecting the very notion of a liberal revolution. Although as a Spanish *ilustrado* he staunchly opposed absolutism, he was also a foe of the democracy represented by the political Patriotic Societies in 1820–1823, when he was founding his Colegio in the Calle San Mateo. Thus Lista is a perfect emblematic link between authoritarian liberalism and historical Romanticism.

Beginning with his first newspaper articles in Seville, Lista's political objective was to propound *moderantismo* as a point of stability between the "horrible despotism" of absolutism, and the "ferocious and bloody licence of the democracies."[37] As a moderate liberal he supported a "Monarchy tempered by representative government." The constitutional régime he envisioned was to consist of three parts: representative government proper, public opinion, and the "sabios" who were intended to mold public opinion. The key element was the last, since public opinion, as he wrote, "is at once what energizes and maintains the balance between the power of government and the freedom of the citizens" (151).

This emphasis on "sabios" reflected Lista's Enlightenment confidence in the intelligentsia, only now, as Elorza notes, his Enlightenment ideals faced the revolutionary situation of post–War of Independence Spain; and here what was needed was a political system that avoided the mistakes in France. According to Lista all attempts to render monarchy and democracy compatible must be resisted. Any kind of political association, and any participation by the "pueblo," would only lead to a Republic and to anarchy. Hence all political associations were to be proscribed, as were all pretexts for the transmission of democratic ideas. As Lista wrote in *El Censor* in 1820, "Haranguing in meetings does not serve to illustrate and correct opinion . . . ; because it does not speak to reason but to the passions; it clouds the spirit and excites the imagination, without teaching or illuminating the understanding" (157). The only public vehicle of expression he excepted was the press, which was to be under prior censorship.

A fundamental premise of Lista's design was to keep the "pueblo" in check. The latter's sole democratic opportunity came when elections were held. Otherwise, it was the passive recipient of whatever "public opinion" the "sabios" helped to create. Thus Lista's polity incorporated a sharp division based on education between the "sabios," trained to form public opinion, and the rest who were not so trained. Only students of "letras" could learn the required ideas and the oratorical skills for their exposition. This was perfectly expressed in the prospectus that Lista wrote for the Colegio de San Mateo: "A nation governed by liberal principles needs above all that the young acquire science and virtue; without these they will neither love constitutionality, which replaces the passions and favoritism with justice, nor be useful to the fatherland or to themselves; because in free governments the uneducated man is of little use and the virtueless man is a danger."[38]

In this way Lista's liberalism promised a controlled political and civil order for the combined classes that directed society. According to Elorza, these included the conservative, the enlightened, the industrial, and the propertied classes, all of whom were interested in defending an order based on property, and not averse to negotiations with the remnants of feudal society. Lista believed that with a monarchy tempered by representative government the bourgeoisie would be able to guarantee the general well-being, and would themselves gradually evolve in the direction of the nobility. The bourgeoisie and the nobility could then address their common political problem: how—in Elorza's words—to "guarantee mechanisms of exclusion vis-à-vis any alternate popular power."[39] In theory and practice, then, Lista and Gómez Hermosilla, author of both *El Jacobinismo* (1823) and a widely used manual of rhetoric, supported Martínez de la Rosa's *Estatuto Real* of 1833–1835, which certified this very peculiar entente between the new middle classes and the nobility, while excluding "popular" participation. But the *Estatuto Real*, we must remember, was also enthusiastically welcomed by Larra, Espronceda, and other "romantics."

As an *ilustrado*, Lista's aesthetic ideas reflected and reinforced his political ones. But if Lista's aristocratic political thought drew on the American Revolution, Bentham, Constant, and Guizot, his aesthetic ideas were meager by comparison. According to Juretschke, Lista let himself be guided by Batteaux and Blair—especially Hugh Blair. In February 1816 he wrote to his friend Reinoso that the latter should base a humanities course on Blair's *Lectures on Rhetoric and Belles Lettres*.[40] The program was to include theories of beauty, genius, and taste, not to mention the "luminous" principle of imitation dear to Batteaux. In fact, faithful to his Enlightenment training, Lista's treatment of poetry was strictly classical and rhetorical. As Juretschke says, he believed in art, not spontaneity, in imitation, not originality, and in inspiration con-trolled by reason. Poetry should depict the "beautiful and sublime" so as to "delight the imagination" and "move the heart." Throughout his life Lista used the critical terms *beauty, sublime, imitation, enthusiasm,* and *genius,* but never conceded any "creative" role to the imagination. Rather like Batteaux he believed genius could only rearrange what was already in nature. Thus, even a poet's fictions were "composed by the imagination as the chemist breaks things down . . . , and recomposes them according to certain laws, without creating new elements").[41]

It was ironic that circumstances conspired to make this revered *ilustrado* a key ideologue between 1820 and 1840, and especially between 1820 and 1826 when Espronceda studied at his Colegio de San Mateo, and Mesonero Romanos and Larra joined his circle. But in 1820–1823 Quintana held the government post of Director General of Schools, while Angel Saavedra and Martínez de la Rosa were involved in politics.[42] This made Lista, as Marrast remarks, with his teaching at the Colegio, his Lectures on Spanish Literature in the Madrid Ateneo, and his editorship of *El Censor* (1820–1822), the most immediate literary (and political) mentor of Espronceda's generation.

Throughout the long period of his ascendancy the only significant literary alteration in Lista's thinking was his eventual acceptance around 1828 of the ideas of A. W. Schlegel, which were central to historical Romanticism. Earlier, in the Trienio Liberal, he believed that these ideas could only lead to anarchy. For instance, in 1821 he wrote, apparently contradicting Schlegel, that one loved Shakespeare and Calderón despite their defects, not because of them. At the same time he rejected the Herderian view that taste was not universal but relative to each country and era. Conflating aesthetics and politics, he concluded: "In taste as in politics one must avoid servile submission as well as unbridled licence. Let us break unimportant rules; but obey the laws of nature and reason." As Marrast notes, "Once again, aesthetics appears to be defined in relation to the social order."[43]

If the literary historical ideas of A. W. Schlegel first came to Lista's attention during the Böhl de Faber–J. Joaquín de Mora debate, it was through Agustín Durán that Lista finally came to accept them. Lista and Durán were in close contact when, in 1828, Durán published the first volume of his *Romancero* and an important *Discurso* in which he maintained that Golden Age theater contained a fundamental expression of Spain's national genius.[44] As a result, besides softening his opposition to historical Romanticism, Lista for the first time criticized the kind of neoclassical rules found in Martínez de la Rosa's 1827 *Poetics*.

Finally, between 1834 and 1836, having assimilated Schlegelian historical Romanticism, Lista began to chastise the French romantic drama of Hugo and Dumas. He now believed that the only "good" romanticism was inward looking, nationalistic, Catholic, and medieval, in short, a historical Romanticism, whereas the depravity of French plays like Alexandre Dumas's *Anthony* showed that they were not romantic but "monstrous."[45]

Flitter and other critics have wondered if Lista's final acceptance of historical Romanticism was not in bad faith.[46] But one could also argue that, instead of political expediency, Lista's change of heart was a sign of intellectual integrity. If, politically and literarily, he finally came to appreciate the tenets of historical Romanticism, it was because they blended with his deeply felt romantic nationalism. This point was not lost on Marrast, who observes that once Lista saw that it was impossible to return to absolutism, he centered his political thought on "the glorification of national tradition."[47] Indeed, Marrast also seems to have read Lista's embrace of historical Romanticism in the light of Vicens Vives's essay. Speaking of the Lista of 1831, Marrast says that he "also reclaims Schlegel's image of 'romantic Spain,' because that was the image traditionalist reformers—of which he was one and who were then directing national politics—wanted to offer Europe and impose on Spaniards to keep them apart from revolutionary tendencies."[48]

Finally, in a further anticipation of Flitter, Marrast suggests that the common denominator of the romanticisms of Böhl de Faber, López Soler, of Durán, and, after 1828, of Lista was the "renewed esteem for Spain's literary patrimony, its historic greatness and its religious tradition" (234).

However, as Flitter says, if Lista and other *moderado* theoreticians were decidedly "historicist" where the Spanish past was concerned, they were still reluctant to apply historicism to the present.

* * *

Critics consider Espronceda the perfect example of the Liberal exile who returned to Spain after the death of Fernando VII in 1833 with a fully developed high romanticism in tow. Instead I suggest we view him as a "sabio," educated according to Lista's political-moral-literary *reformista* agenda. To begin with, both Espronceda's long-term literary project, the epic *Pelayo*, and his compliant postexile subscription in 1835–1836 to the troubadouresque-picturesque romanticism of *El Artista* suggest the degree to which he was influenced by Lista and the Colegio de San Mateo. Marrast has shown that as late as 1836 Espronceda still subscribed to a neoclassically inflected historical Romanticism. It seems reasonable, then, to suppose a similar mixture of conservative aesthetics and politics in both disciple and master.

As the returning exiles realized in 1833–1834, one outstanding change in Madrid was the proliferation of newspapers under the post-absolutist, Cea Bermúdez government. Recall that the parliamentary monarchy projected by Lista entailed a relative freedom of the press. And now with a constitutional monarchy and liberals running the government, there was again the "threat" of democracy. Lista and others feared that, as in the Trienio Liberal, any spread of "democratic" ideas among the masses might incite them to anarchy. Therefore, with perfect coherence, Lista, Sebastián de Miñano, and Javier de Burgos set about corrupting the best young romantics by offering them posts on the new editorial staffs. To this end Javier de Burgos made Estébanez Calderón editor of the *Diario de la administración* by decree. Lista, who became editor-in-chief of the *Gaceta de Madrid* in 1833, brought his disciple Eugenio de Ochoa into the paper in March 1834, and by December 5 Ochoa had advanced to the post of "redactor primero."[49] Finally, Lista, together with Miñano, became editor of *La Estrella, periódico de política, literatura e industria*, which Cea Bermúdez secretly financed to defend his government's conservative policies.

Meanwhile, Espronceda, Ventura de la Vega, Ros de Olano, and Bernardino Nuñez de Arenas were rewarded with *their* newspaper, *El Siglo*. According to Rodríguez-Solís, an early Espronceda biographer, the persons who "inspired and mentored" the newspaper were Quintana, Lista, and the Duque de Frías. Since *El Siglo* attacked the policies that were now being defended by Lista from the less liberal editorship of *La Estrella*, it might appear that Espronceda and company had escaped the older generation's control.[50] However, the Duque de Frías was placed on their editorial board as occasional contributor and censor.[51] But Lista's hold on the young writers showed in other ways as well. For example, the only essay on aesthetics to appear in *El Siglo*, "Influencia del gobierno sobre la poesía" (28 February 1834), and which is attributed to Espronceda, ends with words that the older Lista might have written: "In politics as in poetry, perfection lies in reconciling the greatest amount of liberty with the greatest amount of order possible."[52] This was precisely the balance that characterized the conservative-liberal political credo of *moderantismo*.

The critical consensus is that Lista's literary-political influence on Espronceda had waned by 1836 when he published the first installment of *El Estudiante de Salamanca* (1840); and a parallel belief exists that here and in *El diablo mundo* (1840–1841) a high romantic Espronceda makes an appearance. Against these views, I suggest that even in his last great poems Espronceda's craft is still rooted in an eighteenth-century aesthetic epistemology; and not only rooted, but reined in by it. That this was so during the exile is acknowledged by no less an authority than Marrast, who pointed out that the conception of the sublime in the ode "Al Sol" (1830–1831?) owes much to Ossian and neoclassicism.[53] But the main point is that in Espronceda "preromanticism" was pervasive; and, moreover, it was not secondary but central, for it governed his recycling of Gothic-romantic topoi. This can be demonstrated, first, by briefly examining some of the Gothic aspects of Espronceda's most famous poem, *El Estudiante de Salamanca* and, second, by drawing attention to the eighteenth-century (poetic) epistemology that informs both *El Estudiante de Salamanca* and *El diablo mundo*.[54]

Although little is know about Espronceda's reading at home or in exile—Tasso and Voltaire aside—many formerly prohibited foreign authors became available in Spain during the Trienio Liberal. Following 1820 there was a logical desire for more liberal political and religious books, as well as for authors such as Diderot, Rousseau, Montesquieu, Volney, and Laclos, not to mention Voltaire. Thus, even in the subsequent "ominosa década" wildly popular authors like Sir Walter Scott and Ann Radcliffe must have continued to circulate, or could have been acquired anew from abroad. For example, a bookseller in Perpignan, according to Marrast, announced an eighty-two volume edition of Scott in Spanish in 1824, although this sort of project was perhaps undercut when Scott's translation was authorized by a Barcelona censor in 1826.[55]

Now, to judge by *El Estudiante de Salamanca*, Espronceda, like many other Spaniards, was an avid reader of Gothic novels. Or, to put it another way, if this narrative poem, which was Espronceda's contribution to the Don Juan legend, reflects his understanding of Romanticism, then the latter contains a significant Gothic component. As with romanticism itself, there seems to have been a late dehiscence and dissemination of the Gothic mode, perhaps abetted by the inertia of Spain's neoclassicism. In this respect the frontispiece of Manuel José Quintana's *Poesías* (1808) is emblematic: depicted in a picturesque landscape is a small classical temple with a Gothic ruin in the foreground.[56] Indeed, Quintana produced one of the few Gothic irruptions in Spain that scholars acknowledge: his tragedy, *El duque de Viseo* (1801), wherein castles, dungeons, and near-incest are the order of the day. However, it is more likely, as David T. Gies asserts, that *all* Spanish romantic literature rests on a foundation of Gothic narrative.[57]

Although outstanding critics such as Pedro Salinas and Joaquín Casalduero focused on the gnoseological or Satanic aspects of Espronceda's hero, Don Félix de Montemar, the Gothic connotations of the necrophilic consumation at the end of *El Estudiante de Salamanca* should be obvious. Don Félix comes to a horrible end in the embrace of the skeleton of the woman he had dishonored, which is not an improbable Male Gothic ending. Since this supernatural climax is his punishment for seduction and blasphemy, it is hard not to see Don Félix as a Gothic villain, and his victim, Elvira, as a Gothic heroine. As Anne Williams comments, "the Male Gothic plot takes it for granted that a woman's virtue is her most valuable asset and then places her in a situation where it will be threatened or destroyed. Ultimately she may be (must be?) punished as a 'fallen woman.'"[58] This is precisely the liaison that Espronceda has described in *El Estudiante*. And it replicates "Espronceda's" poetic relations with "Jarifa" and "Teresa," and with his real-life mistress, Teresa Mancha. Of course, in the Male Gothic context, relations such as these also bespeak an anxious, patriarchal fear of the female, and ultimately—in Espronceda's case—of the mother.[59]

In keeping with critics' efforts to read him as a high romantic, much has been made of the Bryonic echoes in El diablo mundo, although they are superficial at best. Instead I want to examine another essential substrate: Espronceda's eighteenth-century (poetic) epistemology. This already makes an appearance at mid-point in El Estudiante de Salamanca, where Espronceda has the macabre figure that Don Félix is pursuing—the skeleton he finally embraces and unveils—personify "the miserable reality" and "the skeleton of this world," but stripped, of course, of its "false colors" ("falsas galas") (vv. 861–864). In other words, Espronceda's ideolect of "illusion" conceals a decidedly preromantic poetics in both poems, in addition to the foregrounded illusion-disillusion dialectic of romantic love.[60]

Espronceda's poetry is post-Newtonian in spirit; God the Creator is often provoked but never appears. Consequently, Espronceda can assume a collaborative eighteenth-century (poetic) epistemology according to which, as proposed by Addison in The Pleasures of Imagination (1712) and developed by James Thomson in his lengthy poem The Seasons (1720s–1740s), "the human mind construct[s] its own aesthetic apprehension of the world."[61] In other words, in Espronceda's two poems, mixed in with the optimistic sense of "illusion" (vv. 789–792) (124), the term is also employed in a technical "perception-nonperception-of-reality" sense (vv. 733–734) (p. 124).[62] What is at issue here is clearest in El diablo mundo: Espronceda has adapted, perhaps from Edward Young's Night Thoughts, the notion of "creative perception," based on the Cartesian and Lockean distinction between primary and secondary properties. God is responsible for providing the former—the world—but man collaborates with his vision by creating the latter.[63] Of course, in El diablo mundo Espronceda is at pains to suggest a loveless illusionless demonic world, so to allegorize the positive, or "illusioned," collaboration between God and Man, he must introduce Faust's counterfigure, Adam, whose unblemished vision is fresh from Paradise. In sum, although Espronceda's last major poems may wear the accoutrements of historical Romanticism, and even at times of high romanticism, their epistemological skeleton is clearly preromantic. Thus, both Espronceda and Lista were drawn to those aspects of historical Romanticism not incompatible with their basic Enlightenment aesthetic.

At the very end of his life Espronceda won a seat to the Cortes as a Republican, but throughout his political life he mediated between constitutional monarchy (Enlightenment reason) and the masses (passion or feeling). And his poetry, which often enacted the same tension between reason and feeling (see *El Estudiante*, vv. 789–792), reflected his political life. That is, Lista's eighteenth-century model of the "faculties" from his poetic psychology was just as present in his own and his disciple's political views. In other words, Espronceda worked to configure public opinion very much as Lista had intended his young "sabios" to do. For instance, in September 1835, only five years after he was supposed to have fought on the Paris barricades, Espronceda traveled on behalf of the Mendizábal government (then busy co-opting intellectuals by promising a revision of the *Estatuto Real*), to the town of Manzanares as emissary to the Conde de las Navas, who was spokesman and military leader of a recalcitrant "Junta central" representing Málaga, Granada, Almería and Jaén.[64]

* * *

These first two sections of chapter 1, on a heretofore underrated historical Romanticism and its use as a *moderado* strategy of legitimation, have offered a different master narrative regarding Spanish Romanticism, centered on a heretofore underrated historical Romanticism and its employment as a *moderado* strategy of legitimation. This new account should help explain the ambiguous nature of Spanish romanticism between 1834 and 1844, as well as its later attenuated development as extreme national-romanticism and as the paler Biedermeier between 1844 and 1868. In the next two sections I will examine select subsequent moments when romantic nationalism, the transhistorical component of historical Romanticism, is especially evident.

In addition to the scattered manifestations of a patriotic romantic nationalism—which shows in the "aggressive and intolerant" mien (Marrast) of the popular *Semanario Pintoresco Español* (1836–1859)—once historical Romanticism became submerged in its legitimating role, Flitter shows that its Herderian historicism shifted toward the present. Thus, after 1833, both Lista and Larra seemed to take cognizance of a potentially negative or positive relationship between society and contemporary literature. For example, while Lista attacked the pessimism of contemporary literature, he considered it an inevitable consequence of eighteenth-century materialism; whereas Larra waxed optimistic about contemporary literature as the enlightened interpreter of moral truths to

society. This application of historicism to the present also helped reconcile Enrique Gil y Carrasco to as unorthodox a work as Espronceda's *El
Estudiante de Salamanca*; according to Flitter, he saw it as the inevitable
poetic expression of unfortunate (but widespread) contemporary philosophical and religious anxieties.

In this way, despite Larra's suicide in 1837, and Lista's superannuated
influence, a more optimistic and contemporary-minded application of the
latent reserves of historicism in historical Romanticism began to make
inroads. Now it became fashionable to stress the "regenerational" aspects
of contemporary or "romantic" literature, by analogy with the earlier
"eighteenth century" enthusiasm for revalidating the literary past. Thus
Manuel Cañete, in an 1848 Ateneo lecture, praised "romanticism" as
"'our literature of regeneration,' [and] as a return to characteristically
national forms of expression."[65] And the notion of romanticism as "social
regeneration" also appeared in the newspaper *No me olvides*, which in
May 1837 took over the defense of romanticism from *El Artista*. Together
with this regenerationism there also appeared a new idealistic conception
of the poet as alienated and yet sensitive, struggling on behalf of society
against the materialism of his day with pen and—curiously—sword. As
Jacinto de Salas Quiroga editorialized in *No me olvides*, romanticism was
viewed as "a wellspring of purity and consolation, seed of social virtues,
apt for drying innocent tears, pardoning guilt, the link that will unite all
beings"(136). This figure of the poet as altruistic idealist will reappear in
Bécquer's prose and poetry in the second half of the century. Not only
that, but, as Flitter remarks, Salas Quiroga's "phraseology immediately
suggests a linkage both with the idealistic premises of Spanish Krausism
and with the concept of 'spiritual doctors' favored by Azorín, Ganivet,
and other intellectuals of the Generation of 1898" (137).

National-Romanticism and Bourgeois Historiography

But before we come to the Generation of 1898, we must pause to
consider the nationalistic historiography of Modesto Lafuente and
Patxot y Ferrer, two of the many romantic historians whose General
Histories of Spain were published between 1840 and 1875.[66] The
General Histories of Modesto Lafuente and Patxot y Ferrer, like those of
Eugenio de Tapia, Eduardo Chao, Cavanilles, Gebhardt, and others,

were the historiographical projection of the goals of the bourgeois revolution in progress. They served—at another level—a series of basic strategic requirements, such as the control of the entire Spanish territory, the introduction of uniformity into a variegated judicial system, and the unification of a fragmented national market, all necessary conditions for the development of a national capitalism.[67] Equally important was their direct promotion among the propertied classes of the notion that they constituted one nation and one people, or rather a single national bourgeoisie.[68] Thus an important task of the Romantic historians was also the creation of a new collective *bourgeois* agent of Spanish history.

A recurrent strategy here was to introduce into past history the ideals of the bourgeois revolution, as if to show that those ideals had always been consubstantially Spanish. This they did by discovering parallels between the bourgeoisie's economic conquest of the state, and the latter's "original" unification under Fernando of Aragón and Isabel I of Castile. Other strategies stressed such "national" efforts as the recent War of Independence. But our present concern is their rewriting of medieval history from a bourgeois point of view. That liberal historians turned with such relish to the Middle Ages was partly due to the Schlegels' "romantic" interest in the Spanish past. For in addition to emphasizing its Christian spirituality, and the revaluation of the *romancero* and Golden Age theater, the Schlegels' message of historicism foregrounded an idealized view of the Middle Ages.[69] That is, Herderian historicism was understood to signify the organic relatedness of Spain's Catholic Middle Ages, its *Romancero*, and its *Poem of the Cid*.

This meant that the historiography dealing with the Middle Ages must reflect the special aura it had acquired, and was acquiring, in countless historical novels and plays that teemed with idealized medieval characters, customs, and architecture. Against such a theatrical backdrop the heroic accomplishments of knights and troubadours offered a gratifying substitute for the brutal prose of daily nineteenth-century life. At the same time, this romantic historiography also incorporated a novelesque proximity of present and past that rendered a faithful historical collation of the two beside the point.[70]

Earlier, the romantic nationalism that had originated within historical Romanticism, and had only amounted to the defensive past-encoded promotion of the present, seemed relatively indifferent to questions of national identity and national unity. But if the historical Romanticism of 1814 to 1844 had treated the past as little more than an aesthetic appendage of the present, by early mid-century the bourgeois agenda was more complex. For example, during the apogee of moderantism, between 1834 and 1854, when the problem of national unification was crucial in Italy and Germany, Spanish liberals took it for granted. Jover Zamora attributes this unconcern about national unity and identity to a [false?] sense of security about the notions of independence, liberty, and unity, garnered in the War of Independence and the Carlist Wars but perhaps also explained by the Jacobine centralization of the state on the Castilian model.[71] By contrast, between 1840 and 1875, particularly between 1854 and 1868, when a more extreme "national-romanticism" occurred, there was "a crescendo of *sui generis* backward-looking nationalism, bent on acquiring prestige"(148). It was not by chance that this period from 1840 to 1875 was when the most successful General Histories of Spain were written, published, and read.

The mid-century "*crescendo*" of centralism and nationalism in Spain was caused by liberal pressures on *moderantismo*, and by the local echoes of 1848. These pressures only increased until in 1868 they produced Spain's own revolution, called "La Gloriosa."[72] Significantly, a parallel increase in patriotic national-romanticism figured in the late romantic theater. Much more popular than either Rivas's *Don Alvaro* (1835) or Zorrilla's *Don Juan Tenorio* (1844) was García Gutiérrez's jingoistic *Venganza catalana*, which in 1864 enjoyed a record fifty-six consecutive performances.[73] Thus, as Jover Zamora implies, a major force behind Modesto Lafuente's history writing was the conservative retrenchment around O'Donnell's Liberal Union Party in the 1860s; the justification for this Union Party, as he says, "seems to have been the *aggiornamento* of historical moderantism so as to include in it two powerful forces of the period: ascendent capitalism and liberalism which, in Spain as in Europe, struggled to impress their mark on the period."[74]

The complexity of this demand for a historically respectable bourgeois rationale probably explains, then, the great number of General Histories that appeared in Spain beginning in the 1840s. But the most successful of these was the *Historia General de España* (1844–1856) by Modesto Lafuente, who belonged, like Espronceda, to the second romantic generation. As Jover Zamora says, the new romantic historiographical consciousness was obviously a patriotic response to foreign histories like S. A. Dunham's *The History of Spain and Portugal* (1832) and Louis Romney's *Histoire d'Espagne depuis les premiers temps jusqu'a nos jours* (1839–1850) (153–154). Indeed, the first romantic history took the form of an annotated Spanish edition of Dunham, by the first-generation romantic politicians Alcalá Galiano, Donoso Cortés, and Martínez de la Rosa (1844–1846).

Besides Modesto Lafuente's single-handed thirty-volume effort, there were other liberal and even traditionalist histories that opposed his perspective.[75] The history by Eduardo Chao (1848–1851) represented a Democratic, even a Republican, point of view. But the most interesting dissident among liberal historians was Francisco Patxot y Ferrer, a confirmed federalist, and one of the first Iberianists, who published his six-volume history between 1857 and 1859.

Because this material is copious, we can only suggest a few of the differences between these historians in conveying a similar bourgeois message. First, liberal romantic historians all agreed that the nation should be "legislatively and politically a single unit, united in religion, with a single national identity, and of course territorial sovereignty."[76] Second, they also were eager to make it seem that the nineteenth-century phenomenon of nationhood had always existed in its present (bourgeois) form.[77] And third, they wanted to make it seem that "the new [bourgeois] revolutionary event [also] dated from time immemorial."[78] As liberal historians they were partial to the periods that seemed to ratify the values they favored. Thus, they were especially eloquent on the Visigothic monarchy, the Muslim invasion of Spain, the joint reign of Fernando and Isabel, the Enlightenment under the Bourbons, and the recent War of Independence.

At the same time, we must underline the victory, within the liberal camp, of the stronger *moderado* point of view over those of more politically progressive historians, particularly on the question of the antiquity of the nation's unification. Since centralism was now an important issue, this victory by *moderado* historians only reconfirmed the existing Castile-centric interpretation of medieval Spanish history.[79] But this importance of centralism and nationalism at mid-century also enforced the gradual erasure of the work of the Republican, federalist, and Iberianist historians, who favored a pluri-nationalism and envisioned some role for the

masses. Two examples regarding the Middle Ages will serve to character-
ize this variety within the general liberal consensus.

According to Modesto Lafuente, Eduardo Chao and others, with the
establishment of the Visigothic monarchy in Toledo, Spain ceased to be
a Roman province and became an independent nation. It thus acquired,
according to Modesto Lafuente, "a nationality and a throne that it had
not had."[80] From this perspective, however, because the Muslim invasion
would then have shattered a pre-existing "national" unity, the Asturian
king, Pelayo, became a symbol of the restoration of this unity through
the "Reconquest."

But certain Democratic and Progressive historians, with a less centralist agenda, held opposing "Iberianist" views of the original Visigothic
invasion; they bridled at the extreme romantic nationalism of the conservative-liberal view, with its combination of centralism, nationalism,
and Catholicism. For example, the Menorcan Patxot y Ferrer found
especially repugnant the instrumentalization of Catholicism by those of
moderado persuasion. He complained that since the 1851 Concordat that
Martínez de la Rosa signed with the Vatican, the Spanish Church supported the exclusive interests of the bourgeoisie.[81]

However, on the central question of Spain's origins as a "nation,"
Patxot's position, although different, was as "Providentalist" as Modesto
Lafuente's. According to Patxot Spain's national identity was due to an
original pre-Roman Iberia. Thus, in his opinion the Roman and
Visigothic dominations were equally instances of "national enslavement."
Yet, curiously, he never questioned the importance of the Reconquest
itself, which, even as an anti–neo-Visigothist,[82] he viewed in a positive
light, since it meant the recovery of the original unity of ancient Iberia.
According to Patxot y Ferrer, "The dislike of the Iberian *pueblo* [for the
Visigoths] became clear . . . when the Arabs entered Spain. Instead of
defending their lords the serfs were happy to change masters. Thus the
Iberian race was reborn in the upper reaches of the Pyrenees, bragging
neither of a Gothic ancestry, nor of continuing a Monarchy that had collapsed amid the jeers of its subjects, but reviving instead the ancient tribal
spirit, creating new rulers, and giving new life to a torpid existence."[83]
This was Patxot's way of implying that a Spanish federalism, the organiza-
tional model preferred by most Republicans and some Progressives, was
every bit as "Spanish" as the *moderado*'s centralist model.

At the same time, despite other differences, a moderate like Modesto Lafuente and a federalist-Iberianist like Patxot y Ferrer agreed on the twin pillars of modern Spanish historiography: first, that Spain's nation-building began with the Reconquest; and second, that the driving force behind this national renaissance was the innate resilience of an "originally Iberian" "Spanish" people. As the authors of *Historiografía y nacionalismo* suggest, the creation of the new bourgeois human agent of Spanish history required the myth of an originary national character. As they explain, "Hispanic uniqueness was lost in pre-history, it could not be dated. This was the . . . national reality that particularized Spaniards and set them apart."[84] In this way a fictional Hispanic identity was projected so far into the past that its true origins became unfathomable. The aim was to prepare an imaginary space on which to write the newly created bourgeois ethos. Hence, this transhistorical "Spanish national character," which coincided with the bourgeois agent of history, was also projected into the past. It was this historiographical manipulation that later enabled Ramón Menéndez Pidal (1869–1968) to rediscover as if by magic a bourgeois "individualism" thumping in the medieval breast of Spain's epic hero, "Cidi" Rodrigo de Vivar.

But the fictive relation to the past implicit in romantic nationalism had another important consequence. Jover Zamora calls it a blatant "disjunction between 'national history' and any 'national project.'"[85] Accordingly, what made Spain exceptional in a European context was its "entirely retrospective" official nineteenth-century historiography. Apparently, romantic historiography continued to be saddled with the original retrospective mode of Herderian historicism. At least there is little trace of a connection between national history and any present or future national project. On the contrary, Jover Zamora observes, "what whetted the historiographical appetite of late Romanticism [was] the grandiose history of the past, distant and heterogeneous with respect to the present, but replete with themes like the Reconquest, Fernando and Isabel I, the Inquisition, etc. Themes admirably suited to fomenting a nationalistic *pathos*; but whose absolute separation from the real historical horizon of Spain to which we refer is obvious" (166–167).

In this way the fusion of moderantism and Liberal Unionism with the Spanish past paralleled the liberals' earlier post-1833 symbiosis with the monarchy, and can only be explained as an obsessive search for historical

respectability (167). Indeed, the romantic historians, like the early historical Romantics, were cathected on the past and chary about its overt
connections with present and future. To judge from their treatment of
history, *moderantismo* and Liberal Unionism had other priorities, namely,
"to consolidate and make sacrosanct a unitary, centralized State focused
on two goals: to guarantee public order and foment material wealth, the
former so as to make certain of the latter" (168–169).

Accustomed as we are to the rhetorical verve of nineteenth-century
European historiography, the unsubtle distortions of the *moderado*-
Liberal Unionist, "*españolista*" perspective should still give us pause. It is
true that the other dissenting republican, federalist, and Iberianist views
could not have been expected to prosper, given the hegemony of the
authoritarian liberal faction between 1843 and 1868. But, just as in the
case of Spanish romanticism, the version Spanish liberalism offers of
itself is not to be believed.[86] Why, then, has the Castile-centric view of
the Middle Ages survived down to the present? For, however much they
might argue over the general liberal reading of Spanish history, later
Republican and Falangist historians both seem to have embraced some
version of the *moderado* dogma of an immemorially unified and centralized, Castile-led, Catholic nation. Obviously Spanish historiography
remains reluctant to confront and question the continual erasure of
Spain's other nationalities, in spite of what micro-nationalist historians,
such as Patxot y Ferrer, Pi y Margall, V. Almirall, J. Vicens Vives, and
Antoní Jutglar, have written in the last 150 years.

Indeed, the case of Patxot y Ferrer is a preview of the misfortunes of
the modern Valencian ethnographer and federalist, Pere Bosch Gimpera
(1891–1974). From a post-Franco perspective, Patxot's federalism, if not
his Iberianism, seems closer to the truth than the national-Catholicism
and centralism of Modesto Lafuente. But, as with the later controversy
between Bosch Gimpera and Menéndez Pidal, the truth of one's viewpoint was no guarantee of its success. If anything, the views of Bosch
Gimpera in 1937 were less welcome than those of Patxot y Ferrer earlier.
For the Nationalist response, voiced by Menéndez Pidal in 1947, was
that during the Second Republic, "A disintegrative voluptuousness tried
to reorganize Spain the way you reorganize a crock by breaking it on the
curb so as to make as many new containers as there were pieces."[87] Thus
Bosch Gimpera saw his federalist and Iberianist ideas attacked—from a

Castilophile viewpoint—under both the Republican and the Franco governments.

The Neoromantic Nationalism of 1898

"Porque Castilla fue fuerza, decencia y mesura,
España existe aún como categoría histórica."—Américo Castro[88]

We turn now to the "Generation of 1898"—Azorín, Unamuno, Antonio and Manuel Machado, and Ramiro de Maeztu—and to its important epigones: José Ortega y Gasset, Ramón Menéndez Pidal, and Américo Castro. In this section I suggest a corrective micro-national perspective on these writers, to supplement the readings offered by P. Lain Entralgo in *La Generación del Noventa y Ocho* (1945), and C. Blanco Aguinaga in *La juventud del 98* (1970). By showing that most of its members were also "organic intellectuals" within the Castile-centric tradition of romantic nationalism, I also respond to Edmund L. King's notion that Unamuno, Azorín, Baroja, and Machado are the *high* romantic generation that Spain never had. Actually, what little proof Edmund L. King offers on behalf of his contention actually supports my own view. This is especially so when he invites us to accept the following as evidence for a late Spanish high romanticism:

> Only when the premises of Romanticism had been deeply established in the Spanish soul could it make reason and history its servants. Azorín could meditate upon the physical and historical texture of Castile. Antonio Machado could write his poems about the *Campos de Castilla*. Unamuno could preach the search for truth in life and the search for life in truth, the doctrine of "within!" (*adentro*), . . . the example of *Obermann*, the meaning of the inner history of Spain, etcetera.[89]

It seems to me that instead of supporting the existence of a late high romantic movement in Spain, Edmund King's evidence begins to expose the ideological thrust of the Generation of 1898's particular variety of romantic nationalism and centralism. This, in turn, may help explain the continued prestige today of this generation of writers and of the period concept, "Generation of 1898," itself, for it has been virtually uncontested since it was advanced in 1913, first by Ortega y Gasset and then by Azorín.[90] As we know, the intellectual prestige of the "Generation of 1898" only increased among Republican exiles after the Spanish Civil War. Indeed, with equal zeal, Republican scholars and liberal Falangists worked to stress—Pérez de la Dehesa, Blanco Aguinaga, Inman Fox—or to explain away—Pedro Laín Entralgo—this generation's youthful political dissent. And even today, Antonio Machado and Ortega y Gasset play fundamental talismanic roles in Spain's cultural politics. This continuing popularity is difficult to account for unless we recall that the writers of 1898 were "regenerationists," that is, modern proponents of a late nineteenth-century Castile-centric romantic nationalism.

Their "universal" literary significance, vaunted by exiled republican academics, has also helped disguise the extent to which their promotion was always ideologically and politically motivated. They were acclaimed—and seem to have escaped any criticism—because following the Civil War their work could be read as an encoded vindication of profound bourgeois nationalist and centralist sentiments, which had first appeared among Liberals with the Carlist Wars, then increased in reaction to the late nineteenth-century political surges of Spain's peripheral micro-nationalisms. In its turn, this micro-nationalist irruption was the political result of the economic and cultural development of Spain's northern coastal regions that dated from the late eighteenth-century. Therefore, the broad appeal of the 98ers—with liberal Falangists, Republicans, and the Spanish Left—is not unrelated to the fact that they were reacting to a threatened national *disunity* with their own collective sublimation of the myth of a spiritually unifying, "essentialist," Castile.

Once we recognize the Castile-centric family resemblances among the *medieval* falsification of a neo-Visigothic tradition, hear the romantic *moderado* inflection of nineteenth-century historiography, and consider the writings of the Generation of 1898, the inherent centralist bias in much of today's criticism of Spain's micro-nationalisms is explained.[91] For most of the nationalist myths for which Castile-centric writers criticize micro-nationalists are mimetic variations on the centralist myths of Spanish state-nationalism. Indeed, in keeping with this center-periphery dialectic, Basque nationalism, today the most intransigent of Spain's

peripheral nationalisms, seems both to replicate Spain's centrifugal problems within its own territory and to represent for centralist Spain what
Fredric Jameson might call the return of the politically repressed.
Inasmuch as the "Castilian" origins of Spain are linguistically and ethni-
cally (as well as mythically) intertwined with a historically verifiable,
non-mythical, region called Vasconia.

In brief, a more searching interpretation of the Generation of 1898
would conclude: (1) that from Joaquín Costa and Angel Ganivet and to
Ramón Menéndez Pidal, José Ortega y Gasset, and Américo Castro,
these writers purveyed a neo-Visigothic, Castilophile version of medieval
Spanish history;[92] (2) that "aesthetically" they articulated an
"*españolista*" millenniumism, with an aversion to the "modern" similar to
those in late Catalán, Basque, Galician, and Aragonese romanticism;
and (3) that they were an important link in the tradition of Castile-centric romantic nationalism, galvanized by the late nineteenth-century
Catalán and Basque economic, cultural, and political resurgences. Thus
the part that fell to these fin-de-siècle writers, as the rusty machine of
the Restoration ground to a halt, was to reinvent the cultural-political,
"intra-historical" or "organic" illusion of a united Spain, not as that
union had been precariously enacted under Fernando and Isabel I, or
reaffirmed under Felipe V and Olivares in 1716 (the so-called Nueva
Planta), but as rewritten between 1840 and 1870 by liberal historians,
anxious to "naturalize" an ever-about-to-be-completed bourgeois revolution in Spain.

Indeed, once Spanish *moderado* liberalism had received its rationale
from "progressive" *afrancesados* like Alberto Lista, Sebastian de Miñano,
and Gómez Hermosilla, it never ceased shifting to the right, ever sensitive to the successive counter-thrusts of dissenting elite Exaltados,
Republicans, Democrats, and Federalists, as well as later foreign and
domestically inspired proletarian movements. This is not to condemn
the stopgap, catch-up Second Republic military, social, and administrative reforms of the Azaña government; it is to suggest that on a deeper
level their perennial liberal oligarchic brand of democracy was vitiated
by its historical origins—namely, the elitist and authoritarian contradictions of Spanish liberalism.[93]

This being the case, the absence of any sustained ideological critique
of the "Generation of 1898" as a group is less difficult to explain. They

have escaped historico-literary revision *because* their spiritualized Castile-centric nationalism provided a rationale for the positions of Republican, Leftist, and Falangist intellectuals after the Civil War. The virtual absence of any socio-critique is especially surprising since their spiritualized Castile-centric nationalism was also the cornerstone of a vast corpus of journalistic social and literary criticism—which has been the object of so much scholarly attention.

Whenever Azorín or Ortega y Gasset attribute intrinsic literary value to an aspect of Spanish culture it is because they find that it expresses the Castile-centric conception of Spain's national spirit, and hence confirms their prior view of the value of "Spanish" nationhood. Reciprocally, canonical "Spanish" literature and other cultural artifacts maintain their exalted status because they were once seen to be animated by these same conceptions and values. Whereas contemporary critics, correctly or not, view the poetry of the post-1914 Spanish Vanguard as "universal" in meaning and appeal, the Generation of 1898 is still esteemed for its reaffirmation of the conservative-liberal Castile-centric spiritual values in literature and nationhood. And with perfect consistency, their Castilophile vision of Spanish culture also implies the progressive repression of other Iberian languages, literatures, oral traditions, and cultural artifacts, as well as the historical erasure of Carlism, Cantonalism, Federalism, pluri-nationalism, bilingualism, and self-determination.

To examine Azorín's uncollected journalistic essays of 1906–1912 is to confirm his affinity with the ideological labors of the romantic poets, novelists, *costumbristas,* and historians of the nineteenth-century.[94] In hundreds of journalistic pieces Azorín maintains that Spanish literature is profound and/or sublime because it preserves and transmits specific national values. Of course, as we have seen, some of these values were to be readily found in the literature because the nineteenth-century writers had recently inscribed them there. This recalls a fundamental precept regarding romantic nation-building: that the "meaning" of a nation's literature is the dominant corporatist ethos of the nation in question.[95]

For instance, in "The Genius of Castile" (ABC, 1912) Azorín praises the way Cervantes combined his "pragmatic sense" and his vision of "the prosaic reality of unpleasant life" with "the idealism of the ancient Books of Chivalry." In another article this Biedermeierish pair, "realism-idealism," reappears as an exclusively Castilian, that is, Spanish, virtue. Azorín professes to see "the essence of Castile" in the character of the Gentleman in *Lazarillo de Tormes* (1554), the first picaresque novel. Or he praises "the nobility of the Castilian day-laborer, [as] root and fundament of a nation" (*La Vanguardia*, 1911), just as Unamuno did.[96]

In addition to meditations on literary icons Azorín, a former Anarchist and soon-to-be-Monarchist, also wrote political essays that anticipate his conservative convictions. For instance, in "Life and Death" (*ABC*, 1911), he addresses the civil and political disarray of Restoration Spain. In view of the corruption and civil disorder that are undermining the nation, he reminds his readers of how King Fernando and Queen Isabel too suffered the slings and arrows of "barons, caciques and oligarchs" until they decided that Spain should be ruled "by one strong . . . inexorable will, dedicated to national prosperity" and forthwith united their kingdoms. "Life and Death" concludes by drawing a clearly anti-democratic but generalized contemporary lesson from Spain's mythic originary unification: the required "labor of purification calls for a strong and decisive will. In this unhinged and anarchic country of ours we must move toward a dictatorial government in order to commence its regeneration."

The most influential university spokesperson for this unsubtle brand of Castile-centric ideology was Ramón Menéndez Pidal, whose historical and literary study of the medieval Spanish epic earned him the directorship of the Real Academia de la Lengua. Throughout his extremely productive life—his first important work, *La epopeya castellana a través de la literatura española*, was published in 1910—Menéndez Pidal stressed the "Castilian" identity of the Spanish epic, which he saw as the original vehicle of a series of "eternal" national traits. Even though the only nearly complete copy of his key text, the *Poem of the Cid*, was originally transcribed (and preserved) by a cleric more Aragonese than Castilian.[97]

As Menéndez Pidal wrote in his essay "Los españoles en la historia": "Historical events do not repeat themselves, but the Man who makes history is ever the same."[98] For this scholar the defining traits of the Spanish Ur-Man were "austerity" ("sobriedad"), "idealism," "individualism," and devoutness ("religiosidad"). In addition, Menéndez Pidal stressed the "popular" spirit of early Spanish literature. As suggested above, this gesture alludes—by negation—to the true abjectness of Spain's rural masses, without the benefit of basic electrification until the 1950s.

Since his "Los españoles en la historia" was originally written to introduce volume 1 of his *Historia General de las literaturas hispánicas* (*General History of Hispanic Literatures*) (1947), it employs a centralist rhetoric of "different but the same." After contrasting the French with the "Castilian-Spanish" family of literature, Menéndez Pidal compares the Castilian-Spanish with the Catalán and Gallego-Portuguese literatures: "The three [began] life with great differences between them, yet without ever contradicting their (Castilian) 'family resemblance,' which makes it impossible to confuse them with other literatures. Naturally, these resemblances not only pertain in the beginning but continue through time."[99]

As we see, the reverse side of this "Castilianization" is an unsubtle downgrading of other Iberian cultures and their ethnia. For example, in "Los españoles," Menéndez Pidal dedicated one section of this famous essay, "Unitedness and Regionalism" ("Unitarismo y regionalism"), to rebutting the pluri-nationalist origin of Spain's "localismo," which was his euphemism for what he recognized was tantamount to national separatist sentiment.[100] In the same section he also attacked the aforementioned ethnographer and former rector of the University of Barcelona, P. Bosch Gimpera, a defender of federalism, who had lectured in Valencia in 1937 on an "authentic Spain constituted by its primitive peoples."[101]

In short, when Ortega y Gasset wrote in *España invertebrada* (1922) that "Castile made Spain and Castile unmade Spain," he was voicing a common liberal postulate. The strength of Ortega's conviction about attaching the fortunes of the Spanish nation-state to those of Castile was only matched by his understandable pessimism about Spain's present and future, a pessimism he shared with members of the Generation of 1898. But the underlying thesis of *España invertebrada* is more nuanced—although Ortega's comparison of Castile's leadership with Cecil Rhodes's invention of Rhodesia is unconsciously revealing. Like Menéndez Pidal, contemporary cultural and political events finally forced Ortega to confront the question of Spain's other historical nationalisms.[102] Indeed, as a good centralist, Ortega was especially exercised by the contemporary national separatist rumblings of Cataláns and Vizcayans (or "*bizcaitar-ras*"). But these were of theoretical interest solely as indices of the modern failure of Castile's leadership of Spain. Just as later in his *La redención de las provincias* (*The Redemption of Provinces*) (1927–1928; 1931), the vitality of Spain's regions, and even of their national separatist movements, in dialectical relation with the Castilian center, were only interesting to Ortega as potential catalysts for an ailing Castile, viewed nonetheless as the soul of Spain. This notion of "Spain as Castile" organizes the essays in *España invertebrada*, but is less noticeable there inasmuch as it appears to refer particularly to the past.[103] However, Ortega agreed in the main with Menéndez Pidal who in 1916 had said: "[Castile] is not all of Spain, but its spirit is the unity of Spain."[104]

As this review indicates, one cannot scrutinize the Generation of 1898's "Castilianization" of Spain without noticing their complementary repression of Iberian national, cultural, and ethnic pluralism—as in Antonio Machado's allusion to the "clamor de mercaderes de muelles de Levante" (the clamor of traders on the docks of Levant).[105] Today, when we read poems by this unimpeachable Republican literary icon, we realize that Castile-centrism and a half-conscious denigration of micronationalism are two sides of the same poet. Once his (and their) sublimation of Castile is relocated within its tradition of romantic nationalism, it becomes easier to reveal the underside of their alleged high romanticism.[106] With this intimation of their exact filiation, instead of diverging authors thematically involved in the *spiritual* regeneration of Spain, it is easier to see them as a "Castilian" intelligentsia defending the "historical category" of a Castile-dominated centripetal Spain, the better to offset the disunity of turn-of-the-century Catalán and Basque micronationalisms. The curious fact is that these writers, who early in their careers were or might have been part of a local national separatist intelligentsia, opted instead for the centralist majority nationalism.

The exception that proves this rule is Ramón María del Valle-Inclán (1866–1936), the Galician writer and lifelong Carlist, whose political "eccentricities" scholars have long sought to exorcise by reinventing him as a *modernista* or as a proto-Marxist.[107] On the contrary, his particular genius was to realize that, as the authors of *Breve historia de España* observe, "the 'Generation of 1898's' famous 'problem of Spain' disguise[d] the collapse of a clearly defined concept of Spain that nevertheless [would] survive into the 1950s."[108]

The Return of the Politically Repressed

To northern European romantics Spain seemed a more heroic, demotic, romantic country than their own; instead it was a raggle-taggle country of painfully separated castes. As the Catalán Valentí Almirall wrote in *L'Espagne telle qu'elle est"* (Paris, 1887), the Spain of foreign romantic sojourners like Théophile Gautier was inhabited by a poverty-ridden and disease-plagued peasantry. Even Ortega y Gasset, as late as 1922, wondered that Spain still had a predominantly serf-like agrarian population, waiting, we must suppose, for their revolution. However, when that revolution finally boiled over in 1934 and 1936–1939, in the guise of a civil war, the ruling elites on both sides conspired—in different ways—to repress it.

Nevertheless, in his *España invertebrada*, Ortega y Gasset also acknowledged that the political stagnation of Restoration Spain was a clear sign of the failure of Castilian leadership. Without precisely reject-ing Ortega's diagnosis of Spain's nineteenth-century political prostration, foreign historians such as Sir Raymond Carr and Richard Herr have been hard put to explain the Restoration's failure to modernize the country.[109] Today it is generally admitted that the idea that authentic liberal advances were obstructed by powerful conservative forces—the "two Spains explanation"—is a self-serving nostrum. Moreover, it was proba-bly launched by the early nineteenth-century liberals who postponed sine die the implementation of Article 3 of the Spanish Declaration of the Rights of Man and Citizens of 1812, which promised that "the sover-eignty of the nation resides in the people." Of course, this postponement soon became a permanent negation, as Jeremy Bentham predicted. Typically, the liberals were soon enacting policies like the *Estatuto Real* of 1834, more in keeping with Enlightened reforms envisioned under the ancien régime.

Because of the massive disenfranchisement of the population—in 1840 only 10 percent of the population could read and write—Liberal, moderate, and even Progressive régimes, were only able to survive by tol-erating a sui generis militarism that originated in their own pre-1820 Liberal attempts to wrest hegemony from the absolutism of Fernando VII. Thus, bourgeois liberals actually invented the now familiar civilian-military pronunciamiento.[110] But, additionally, to secure the societal stability required for economic development, it also fomented a second, administrative militarism—that specialists have named "Praetorianism"—which turned out to be a veritable *institutional displacement of hegemony*, implemented and effected by the Military."[111]

Even with liberal hegemony thus doubly assured, the star of the military continued to rise, in part because of the Carlist and Colonial Wars, in part thanks to its own corporatism. Finally, to insure and maintain a public order and consolidate their fragile victory, the progressive National Militia was disarmed in 1843–1844, and the institutionalized military control of public order by the highly centralized Guardia Civil was decreed in 1844.[112] In short, instead of introducing a classic Liberal European model of citizen safety ("seguridad ciudadana"), Spain's solution was to implant a military model of public order to police the citizenry. Until, as a recent history delicately puts it, "Spain entire began to collapse at the beginning of the XXth century with the explosion of the proletarian masses and the inroads of Catalán nationalism among the middle class."[113]

To understand the extent to which, despite historical Romanticism's contribution, early and late liberal hegemony depended on "Praetorian" support, one has but to examine such studies as *Orden público y militarismo en la España constitucional (1812–1983)* by Manuel Ballbé, *Rey, Cortes y fuerza armada en los orígenes de la España liberal, 1808–1823* by Roberto L. Blanco Valdés, *Cien años de militarismo en España* by Joaquim Lleixà, or *La Guardia Civil y los orígenes del estado centralista* and *El aparato policial en España* by Diego López Garrido. For instance, Ballbé's classic study of public order conveys the sobering message that, ever since the demise of the ancien régime, Spanish governments, whether authoritarian Liberal, non-totalitarian dictatorship, or Republican, although apparently providing acceptable statutory laws of public order, have systematically violated them in letter and spirit. This was necessary to make functional a centralized political system based not on a classical European "universal" suffrage but on the policing of an urban and a rural proletariat, dominated by a narrowly drawn military and professional middle class. In this respect, the title of Ballbé's chapter on the Second Republic (1931–1939), "The Contradictions of the Second Republic and the Creation of an Authoritarian Democracy," is sufficiently eloquent.[114]

Such especially pungent realities as these is what the Manichean "two Spains explanation" of liberal failures was designed to hide. It is why such a tortured explanation was embraced by both victors (Falangist intellectuals) and vanquished (exiled Republicans, Communists, Anarchists) following the Civil War. And today it still obscures: (1) the virtual disenfranchisement of the agrarian and urban masses until after Franco's death; (2) the modern political and cultural dysfunction caused by a political and economic imbalance between a retrograde center and South and a highly industrialized Northern periphery; and (3) the genuine cultural diversity of Spain's ethnic nationalisms, which survived the cultural genocide of the Franco years. The great material and spiritual costs to the nation of this diversity now seem the very heart of the matter.

For, as Richard Herr reminds us, a center-periphery conflict was the only unresolved national "tension" remaining when Franco died in 1975. According to Herr, time and the Generalissimo had solved Spain's other two perennial conflicts—the religious problem and the urban-rural developmental differential. But in the nineteenth and twentieth centuries economic and political aspects of this remaining centrifugal force caused the central government enormous distress. According to Juan Linz, the root of the center-periphery problem in modern times is not the obstreperousness of the micro-nationalisms, but the historical failure of the center to assimilate them. Indeed, if we apply Ernest Gellner's definition of nationalism as the "generalized imposition on a society of a single 'high culture,' where previously the majority enjoyed different 'low culture(s),'"[115] it is obvious that no such overarching nationalism was achieved in Spain. Thus, as Linz says, Spain exemplifies "the early creation of a State where the political, social and cultural integration of its territorial components—its nation-building—was not fully accomplished,"[116] or perhaps a nation in which *the* national culture has been a simulacrum compounded of one-fourth "casticismo"—or profound popular eighteenth-century anti-Enlightenment despair (Vicens Vives)—and three-fourths German, French, Anglo-American, and Spanish romantic fabrication.

With this point we conclude our inscription of "Spanish Romanticism" in the Spanish bourgeoisie's struggle toward state hegemony. If liberal-conservative romantic poets and historians successfully promoted the retrospective illusion of a Spain completely unified under Fernando and Isabel I, nineteenth-century politicians were less successful in consolidating the nation-state—although romantically inclined historians like Modesto Lafuente, dramatists like Zorrilla, poets like Bécquer, and historical novelists like Galdós, gave them every support. The result has been that generations of elite citizens have learned that they are descended from a Visigothic-Castilian aristocracy, that their national literature is quintessentially "democratic" and "popular," that their national theater was not a Valencian but a Castilian creation, and that their national epic, vehicle for their own bourgeois values, could only have been composed by fierce Castilians. Just as Spain's whole imperial enterprise could only have been imagined and executed, according to Ortega y Gasset, by Castilians.[117]

Nevertheless, our genealogy of literary romanticism's part in the invention of modern Spain, has unearthed another, more altruistic, if equally romantic, truth—already envisioned by peripheral nationalists like Patxot y Ferrer and Bosch Gimpera—that Spain's "natural" political configuration is in fact not Castile-centric, but federal. Indeed, the "regionalizing" impulse in the new 1978 Constitution was partly designed to achieve precisely this ideal.

CHAPTER II

Romanticism in Ruins

To interpret romanticism means quite literally to interpret the past as such, *our* past precisely to the extent that we are beings who want to be defined and, as such, interpreted in relation to a totality of experience that slips into the past. The content of this experience is perhaps less important than the fact that we have experienced it *in its passing away*, and that it thereby has contributed in an unmediated way (that is, in the form of an act) to the constitution of our own consciousness of temporality. Now it is precisely this experience of the temporal relation between the act and its interpretation that is one of the main themes of romantic poetry.—Paul de Man[1]

I have argued that during the bourgeois revolutionary cycle in Spain there was a grudging experience of historical Romanticism, but no *high* romantic movement. Because Spain was culturally belated and peripheral, its reception of foreign romanticism coincided with an ongoing compulsion to reinterpret its historical past. My therapy has been to suggest that if politics took the romantic event prisoner, the meager historical Romanticism available intervened importantly, though unsuccessfully, in the invention of modern Spain. In this chapter, besides examining recent theories and interpretations of Spanish and European romanticism, I want to pursue further the aesthetic force of literature on history. This means that the underlying subject of the present chapter, in addition to the interested romantic-specific interpretation of the past, is poetry's potential for disclosing "historicality," an aspect of romantic theory that is only now reaching Spain.[2] Thus, section 1 reviews how the debate at Jena surrounding the juxtaposition of the classical and the modern issued in a distinctly philosophical romanticism. Section 2 shows that in Spain the corresponding controversy was more in the nature of a nationalistic cultur-al-political debate. Section 3 pieces together a Hölderlinesque "his-torical poetics" with which for a time Paul de Man contested the reigning Wellek-Abrams consensus on European high romanticism. Section 4 examines various conflicting attempts to theorize Spanish romanticism, proposing an alternative restitutional solution to the question of high romanticism in Spain.

Therefore, this chapter is centered as much on reinterpreters of romanticism as on its original interpreters.[3] Although for Spanish romanticism a complete list would reach from Böhl de Faber to Derek Flitter, and for European romanticism would reach from Mme. de Stäel to Virgil Nemoianu, I shall be extremely selective. In the process I do not mean to fault Spanish romanticism for its penury and belatedness; on the contrary, I suggest that the difference between the ideological vigor that powered Europe's surfeit of romanticism and Spain's dearth is less than one might think. For the decisive factor here is not only the romanticism itself but the force of its reinterpretation.

This examination of romaniticisms will prepare the way for the next two chapters, on Bécquer's prose and Cernuda's poetry, which together illustrate the ruin and restitution of romanticism in Spain. Remember that there I take the case of Cernuda's poetry to be exem-plary and by no means exceptional. My ultimate aim is to go beyond present notions of Spanish romanticism as a subsystem of the conservative ideology of Spanish liberalism, or as a weak brother/sister of European high romanticism. Indeed, with the identi-fication of the high romanticism in Cernuda's poetry, a new under-standing of Spanish romanticism will emerge. For the praxis of his poetry enlightens us as no critique of theories *about* romanticism possibly can.

Originary "Messianic" Romanticism

The secular religious impulse so variously interpreted by later romanticisms originated with the Jena group. According to critics as dif-ferent as Walter Benjamin, Meyer H. Abrams, and Virgil Nemoianu, the strength of this impulse derived from a secularized messianism. As we know, Benjamin salvaged this special character for later critics when he relayed in his doctoral dissertation that "the thought of an ideal humanity perfecting itself ad infinitum is rejected; instead, what is demanded is the 'kingdom of God' now, in time and on earth. . . ."[4] Of course, his dissertation's stated theme was the romantic concept of criticism, and he showed that the Jena circle's treatment of the topics of literature, art, and criticism could be distinguished as a philosophical position from the treatments of Kant and the idealists.[5]

The initial communicants of this new religion were August Wilhelm and Friedrich Schlegel, the former's wife Caroline, Novalis, and Schleiermacher. Their brief intellectual life together was centered in the journal *Athenæum*, published between 1798 and 1800, and their small literary output also included the *Hymns to Night*, the novel *Lucinde*, and the *Monologues*. Usually, the absolute control that this group has exercised over literary romanticism is explained by their elliptical interpretation of the relation of the modern to the classical, a subject that J. J. Winckelmann had treated in his *History of the Art of Antiquity* (1763–1768) and that Schiller and Hölderlin also developed in opposing ways. A second point of particular concern to Friedrich Schlegel was the conversion of the absolute "I" of transcendental idealism into an individual "creative" romantic subject and, consequently, the redirection of speculative philosophy toward the poetic interpretation of subjectivity.[6]

Yet it was the slightly older Schiller, in *On Naive and Sentimental Poetry* (1795–1796), who provided the initial impulse for German romantic theory, as he did with his subsequent speculations regarding the beautiful and the sublime. Indeed, his complex treatment of this antinomic pair contained what turned out to be extremely productive inner contradictions. For, on the one hand, Schiller claimed that man's desire for beauty provides a release from his pure, natural state, although he felt that beauty by itself is insufficient to render man independent of nature. On the other hand, as Schiller later wrote in *The Sublime* (1801), mankind has another, higher destiny that can only be achieved through the agency of the sublime.[7] Although contemplation of beautiful objects provides a sense of freedom, contemplation of nature provides a sense of sublimity—as Kant had said. Thus, in pondering these two values, Schiller eventually reversed his appreciations of them. As Wessell explains:

The ideal for man of harmony as a sensuous-rational being within the limits of nature [was] replaced by the conception of man
as a pure spirit transcending nature, and from this point of view,
beauty [was] judged as inferior.[8]

In a gesture that reveals the imprint of Kant's thinking, Schiller would
now reason that the sublime is superior because of the accompanying
experience of pain that helps humankind overcome a sense of limitations. The feeling of the sublime, he maintained, is liberating because it
is compounded of our feelings of weakness, of our inability to embrace
the object, but also of a feeling of moral superiority, which recognizes no
limitations. Thus, as Schiller said,

> a sublime object, precisely because it thwarts the senses, is suit-
> able with relation to reason, and it gives a joy by means of a
> higher faculty, at the same time that it wounds us in an inferior
> one.[9]

In this way Schiller attempted to establish the superiority of sublimity
over beauty. However, simply as pure ideals, his original categorizations
of both seem self-contradictory. If the highest perfection lies in the beauty of nature, it makes little or no sense to speak of a more perfect sublimity somewhere beyond.[10]

At the same time, Schiller's attempts to resolve these contradictions
led him, in On Naive and Sentimental Poetry, to historicize all his antithetical terms. What had originally been theoretical or symbolic distinc-
tions thereby acquired enormous and unexpected historical leverage.
Beauty and the naive became associated with the type of perfection
already achieved by classical Greece, whereas the sublime and the sentimental became distant, all but impossible perfections sought by the
romantics or moderns. Of critical importance, Greek poetry ceased to be
the only ideal worthy of imitation. So, following Schiller's essays, if the
perfection of classical art continued to represent a desirable absolute,
now there was also a distinct ideal for the romantic or modern era: an
infinite striving after the ideal. Judged by this new criterion, becoming
was deemed superior to being, striving more noble than achievement,

and insatiable longing far superior to the satisfactions of achievement.[11] However, Schiller's delineation of the contrast between the naive and the sentimental (and between the beautiful and the sublime) was unsatisfactory both as antithesis and as synthesis.

In the Preface to his *On the Study of Greek Poetry* (1795) Friedrich Schlegel acknowledged Schiller's influence on his own estimation of Greek poetry. Indeed, according to Wessell, in raising modern poetry to the level of Greek poetry, Schiller had virtually provided Schlegel "with the antipodes of an aesthetic antithesis whose dialectical resolution [eventually] resulted in romanticism."[12] In schematic form, what Friedrich Schlegel went on to achieve was a viable dynamic synthesis in which the antagonistic principles of naive classical poetry and sentimental modern poetry became reconciled. In this way, the "romanticism" that Friedrich Schlegel deployed in the *Lyceum*, the *Athenæum*, and the *Ideen*, was "the progressive development of [a] balance . . . between nature and culture, life and decadence, ancients and moderns, understanding and reason, individual and universal, and unity and abundance."[13]

In the course of his attempts to coordinate these sets of opposites, Friedrich Schlegel reinterpreted the figure of irony so that it became at once the affirmation and negation of the object and, indeed, a fundamental structural principle of artistic creation that he variously described as an "arabesque" and as "Universal Poetry."[14] According to Friedrich Schlegel, "romantic irony" was a satisfactory articulation of the sought-after synthesis of the classical and the modern that Schiller's lucubrations had failed to produce. However, in addition to giving special importance to criticism, *Witz*, and the literary fragment, and affirming that love and the idyll were the only means of achieving a perfect, totalized subjectivity,[15] Schlegel also served would-be romantics with a daunting challenge: he asked them to measure themselves against such works as Goethe's *Wilhelm Meister*, and to compete with "the very best of modern poetry," *The Divine Comedy* and *Don Quijote*.

In this way, Friedrich Schlegel's conceptual steps beyond Schiller provoked several unexpected reincarnations of speculative philosophy: as the work of art in later romanticism, as dramatic theory in Hölderlin, and as idealism in Hegel. Philippe Lacoue-Labarthe and Jean-Luc Nancy have made these permutations the object of a strictly philosophical read-ing of the basic romantic texts of the *Athenæum*.[16] Their purpose is to deemphasize the pseudo-religious messianism in Jena romanticism and to refocus on its philosophical separation from post-Fichtean idealism.

Their Benjaminian view is that the *Athenæum* texts are not literary theory about classical versus modern at all, but rightly understood as "theory itself [become] literature."[17] Lacoue-Labarthe and Nancy main-tain that while not exclusively philosophical, a proper understanding of romanticism must involve its originary relationship with philosophy. Thus, they reject all subsequent paradigms of this romanticism as harbin-ger of a new sensibility, as an essentially literary movement, or as a development of the Enlightenment or of *Sturm und Drang*. Instead, they maintain that the origin of romanticism was a *"crisis" in* philosophy, of which the essay "Earliest System-Program of German Idealism" (1796)—perhaps co-authored by Hegel, Hölderlin, and Schelling—is a symptom. Of course, this amounts to asserting that the romantics had no predeces-sors, at least not in eighteenth-century aesthetics. They contend that romanticism only became possible once Kant had linked together aes-thetics and philosophy; or once transcendental Aesthetics became a problem for, or *within*, philosophy.[18] Accordingly, they argue that roman-ticism is an event that occurred in the course of seeking a solution to Kant's "problematic of the subject unpresentable to itself."

Lacoue-Labarthe and Nancy believe that the authors of the "Earliest System-Program" attempted to surpass Kant or, rather, to transform his "moral subject" into an ideal subject, "absolutely free and thereby con-scious of itself." In this absolute freedom lay the very possibility of the System, wherein the world was the corollary of the subject as well as its creation, its work.[19] But in the second half of the "Earliest System-Program" romanticism moved away from idealism. For "the philosophy of the Spirit [is] an aesthetic philosophy"—which meant that the "Spirit" or "System-subject" implied a concept of the organic because it was "a *living System*." But "the life implied here [is] *beautiful*, and the organism which it animates or within which it occurs . . . [is] essentially the *work of art*."[20] Thus these "romantics" discovered in art the unity that Kant had been seeking, rather than in politics and the state where Hegel had sought it. According to the "Earliest System-Program," this was why "the philosopher must have as much aesthetic power as the poet" and why "art is the speculative *organon par excellence*."[21] Or, as the translator-editors of *L'absolue littéraire* explain,

> the Jena romantics (along with the romantico-modern period in general) envision the production of the Subject ([or] the Subject's self-production) in the work of art, which is to say, both in the artwork and in its generative or operative productivity (its "creativity"). In one sense, as Lacoue-Labarthe and Nancy point out, Friedrich Schlegel even envisages the completion of philosophy in the work of art. The adequate presentation of the subject is thus accomplished through what Lacoue-Labarthe and Nancy call *eidaesthetics*, or the (attempted) subsumption and presentation of the Idea within the work of art.[22]

In concluding, Lacoue-Labarthe and Nancy suggest, in a section entitled "L'équivoque romantique," that the Jena romantics may be, as well as inventors of "theory as literature," the genuine precursors of Blanchot's, Derrida's, and de Man's *un*deconstructedly *romantic* theories of the "Otherness" of writing.[23]

The Ruins of Spanish Romanticism

Scholars studying Spanish romanticism have often failed to distinguish clearly between romantic theory and theories of romanticism, even though the difference is not inherently difficult to perceive.[24] For if we select Schiller's *On Naive and Sentimental Poetry* as our paradigmatic romantic theory, there is no early programmatic text about Spanish romanticism that resembles it at all. On the other hand, there *are* later texts, such as Bécquer's "Cartas literarias a una mujer" (1860–1861) and Pedro Salinas's *Reality and the Poet in Spanish Poetry* (1940), that do offer a sound basis for comparison.[25] Hispanists, it would seem, have been dealing primarily with theories *about* romanticism—and rather late ones at that—due to the turbulent conditions of Spanish culture in this period. But even earlier, Joseph Addison's *The Pleasures of the Imagination* of 1712 failed to appear in a Spanish translation until 1804.

Additionally, while an admixture of seventeenth- and eighteenth-century European aesthetic ideas was still important in early nineteenth-century Spain, no term has been agreed on to designate this period of transition. There is no term such as *sensibility,* commonly used in studies of English literature, for the period prior to romanticism.[26] Some such term would help reduce the confusion caused by a rococo and a neoclassicism that survive the eighteenth century and mingle with a sui generis proto-romanticism. However, we would then have to decide where to locate the beginning and end of a Spanish era of Sensibility. Or, if we opted for "preromanticism" instead, the "pre-" would have to imply a "not *yet* romanticism" rather than a *"predisposition to* romanticism.[27]Without some such term critics are in danger of continuing to interpret eighteenth-century or preromantic stylemes incorrectly as proof of a Spanish high romanticism.

Indeed, to read such indicators correctly, one must remember that Spanish Enlightenment figures such as Cadalso, Jovellanos, Cienfuegos, Quintana, and Meléndez Valdés, had already incorporated numerous "preromantic" aspects—in the sense just indicated—of Addison, Young, Ossian, Thomson, and Lewis into their works. As Marrast points out, Cadalso, for example, depicted unusual passion in his *Noches lúgubres,* while Quintana reproduced aspects of Monk Lewis's Gothic in his *El duque de Viseo,* in addition to experimenting with a more animated conception of historical figures in his *Vidas de españoles célebres.*[28] Most important, because of his promotion by Hugh Blair, Munárriz, and Quintana, it was Ossian and not Milton who made a characteristic impact on Spanish epic, lyric, and dramatic poetry. Like the French and Italians before them, the Spanish neoclassical poets found Ossian irresistible.[29] However, the difference in Spain lay in a fascination with Ossian that lasted, as in the case of Espronceda, well into the 1830s.[30]

What is more, during the War of Independence (1808–1814) late eighteenth-century writers were forced to chose between two untenable positions, that is, between becoming traditionalists and renouncing their revered French culture or becoming *afrancesados* and betraying their country.[31] Needless to say many appeared to waver, and the political options imposed by the war were reflected in the literature they produced. For example, in response to the French Revolution, Cienfuegos and Quintana wrote "a more radical philosophical poetry" (Derozier), while Lista, the younger Moratín, and Gómez Hermosilla were cowed by the foreign and domestic revolutionary violence. However, as late as the Trienio Liberal older liberal *afrancesados* of the prewar generation were still practicing an enlightened despotism in political and cultural affairs.[32] In this way, as in the literary and political education of Lista's pupils, much of their alleged romanticism was in fact derived from these Spanish Enlightenment figures, and not—directly or even indirectly— from French, German, English, or Italian romantics.[33]

There is a another misstep that has hindered a deeper understanding of romanticism in Spain. There is a too ready acceptance of the notion that the political exiles, returning from London and Paris, inaugurated a liberal high romanticism in Spain. Since exiles that returned following the death of Fernando VII were technically liberals, and since romanticism existed in their places of exile, this claim exhibits a prima facie truth. However, it is easily disproved by scrutinizing the actual composition of the "high" romanticism that these returning exiles professed or exhibited. For example, there is Alcalá Galiano's Preface to Rivas's *El moro expósito* (1834). Once considered an essential manifesto of Spanish romanticism, and proof of these exiles' high romanticism, this essay today is considered poorly informed in comparison with Durán's earlier autocthonous Discurso of 1828.[34]

But the notion of a high romanticism imputed to Espronceda while in exile is even less well founded. As we know, the most colorful aspects of Espronceda's exile, between 1827 and 1833, in Lisbon, London, and Paris, center on his love affair with Teresa Mancha, whom he probably met in Lisbon, pursued to London, and made off with in Paris. But, according to Marrast, present accounts of their affair are due to friendly biographers, whereas French police and Spanish diplomatic records give a considerably less "romantic" account of his comings and goings.[35]

The scant poetry that Espronceda wrote abroad suggests that he remained the intellectual disciple of Alberto Lista throughout his exile. We know that in Paris Espronceda continued work on his *Pelayo*, which Lista had suggested to him when he was seventeen. Centered on the Reconquest, this was a favorite subject among Enlightenment authors such as Jovellanos (*Pelayo*), Quintana (*Pelayo*), and the older Moratín (*Hormesinda*). From Marrast's chronology of the never-completed epic's

piecemeal composition, it is clear that although Espronceda soon deviat-
ed from Lista's outline—refocusing the poem on Sancho, Rodrigo, and
Florinda—his primary sources and poetic models were historical dramas
by Quintana, Martínez de la Rosa, and Angel de Saavedra (later Duque
de Rivas), which were staged during the liberal respite of 1820–1823
before his exile.[36]

This does not mean that Espronceda escaped all foreign influence
during and after his exile. In the fragments of *Pelayo* written abroad, critics have discovered—in addition to the influence of Mariana, Quintana,
and Meléndez Valdés—reflections of Angel de Saavedra's *Florinda* (published 1834), Tasso's *Gerusalemme liberata* and Voltaire's *La Henriade*.
Espronceda's later "octavas" for the poem (Rodrigo's dream, a description
of a seraglio, and a depiction of hunger), published in *El Artista* in
April–May of 1835, appeared with the notation that they were part of "a
work written according to romantic doctrines." But this "romanticism"
was heavily imitative of Ossian and actually, as Robert Marrast puts it, a
"romanticismo histórico-exótico-tenebroso," that in England would have
seemed distinctly archaic.[37]

In fact, it seems that the authors most impressive to Espronceda, as
late as 1828–1832, were neither Lord Byron nor Victor Hugo, but Ossian
and Tasso.[38] For the late *Pelayo* fragments, as well as other poems of
1830–1831, such as "Oscar y Malvina," show the clear imprint of
Ossian.[39] Here was the source of Espronceda's more sentimental attitude
in poetry. In fact, before the celebrated postexile "Canciones" of
1835–1840, there is the certain influence of Lista's flexible neoclassical
aesthetic in most of the poetry Espronceda wrote.[40] That is to say, and we
may take his case as exemplary, though Espronceda may have fought on
the barricades beside French revolutionaries in July 1830, whatever literary romanticism he took home to Madrid had little to do with that of
Victor Hugo, Wordsworth, or Coleridge.

On a European scale, therefore, Espronceda's aesthetic practice in
exile bespeaks instead a distinctly *pre*romantic disposition. And once in
Spain he seems to have easily assimilated the variety of historical
Romanticism already accepted by Lista, by Eugenio de Ochoa, and by
Federico de Madrazo, the editors of *El Artista*. In sum, not only did
Espronceda not return home from exile bearing a liberal high romanti-
cism, but he took up on his return the domestic historical Romanticism

that had been developing in Spain since well before 1833. In this regard, Marrast anticipates a point made by Derek Flitter to the effect that

> Durán, Lista, Bretón, and later Ochoa, accepted with small differences the same primitive, national and historical Romanticism based on Schlegel, although they impose on the writer's freedom the strict limits of national tradition and morality. . . . From this point of view, the writings of Espronceda that appeared after 1834—articles, poems, novels, plays—contain nothing that could be considered [from the viewpoint of historical Romanticism] subversive or perverse.[41]

At the same time, a national obsession with the medieval themes that also affected Espronceda, would continue well after his death, becoming increasingly pronounced between 1840 and the 1868 revolution. This exaggerated fascination with the medieval may have begun with imitations of Sir Walter Scott, but the extraordinary success of García Gutiérrez's jingoistic *Venganza catalana* in 1864 is surely its late apotheosis. In addition to invading the theater, the medieval modality was responsible for other works of national self-congratulation—such as Pablo Piferrer's monumental *Recuerdos y bellezas de España* (1839, 1842) and Gustavo Adolfo Bécquer's *Historia de los templos de España* (1857–1858). But, as Flitter notes, strict "scholarly historical study would be equally indelibly impressed with the romantic vogue for medievalism. . . ."[42] Besides appearing in liberal historiography, other popular manifestations of this romantic nationalism were the *costumbrismo* of Mesonero Romanos and the Biedermeierish novels of Fernán Caballero (Cecilia Böhl de Faber).[43]

In this way, most of the philosophical—and even the historical—implications of Schiller's pairing of the naive and the sentimental and A. W. Schlegel's contrasting of *das Klassisch* and *das Romantische*, although glimpsed by the widely read senior Böhl von Faber, were lost on the historical Romantics. At least, when Lista delivered his influential Ateneo lectures of 1836 he spoke not of "classic" and "romantic," but of "good" versus "bad" literature. By the former he meant, of course, medieval and national, as opposed to French, romanticism.[44] From the beginning, what classicism stood for in Germany held little interest for Spanish historical

Romantics. Moreover, Lista's condemnations of foreign romantic literature carried such weight that Agustín Durán, Alcalá Galiano, and even
Larra finally repudiated Dumas and French romantic theater altogether.
Given Lista's veto, even the name "romantic" was increasingly displaced
by the euphemism "new literature," or by "*romancesco.*" Juretschke documents this self-censorship in Balmes, Quadrado, Borao, Cañete, and
Milá y Fontanals, who, as early as 1842, apologized for calling the novels
of Sir Walter Scott "romantic."[45] As Flitter concludes, "The application
of Herder's framework of national-catholic ideas, although indirect, was
therefore of greater eventual significance than the classical-romantic
polemic itself."[46] And thus Friedrich Schlegel's brilliant synthesis was
lost to romantic theory in Spain. Instead, several successive romantic
generations turned the polemic over romanticism in the direction of
national and literary regeneration.

   The literary critic Gabino Tejado (1819–1891) is a typical expression of the second romantic generation's mismanagement of the classic-
modern debate in Spain. According to Flitter, he praised the Duque de
Rivas for *El moro expósito* and the *Romances históricos* because they
marked a change in his work from sterile imitation to "a profound apprehension of Spanish nationality." The value in romanticism, according to
Tejado, lay in having drawn attention to the fact that Golden Age
drama and the *Romancero* expressed "the feelings and even the moral
philosophy of the nation and of individuals as seen in their pleasures,
beliefs, and inclinations" (177). As with the General Histories of the
romantic historians, instead of being an admonition to the present, the
past was rewritten as its simulacrum. Thus, the past was assimilated to
the present, as in the popular theatrical *refundición*, or else became its
own parody. Significantly, the dominant historicist-influenced mode of
Spanish romanticism was virtually without a consciousness of temporality, of "*being-*historical," that the necessary discontinuities of historical
distance usually promote among romantics.

   This collapsing of historical distance was the reflex of an elite
whose horror of political and social revolution explains to a large extent
the (mis)fortunes of romanticism in Spain, as well as why nineteenth-
century literary culture atrophied in Spain after 1843 and why Spain fell
far short of the national rebirth that occurred in Germany when the
intelligentsia debated its cultural distance from Greece. Further, the

Spanish elite's horror of revolution explains why conservative, nationally acclaimed writers such as Zorrilla and Campoamor enjoyed such extended careers and, finally, why Valera and Clarín, the powerful Restoration literary critics, at first found an innocuous Spanish (or Andalusian) *modernismo* so threatening—just as Alberto Lista and others found French romantic theater threatening fifty years before.

In contrast to the historical Romantics, a Biedermeierish national-romantic, Gustavo Adolfo Bécquer (1836–1870), struggled to manifest a consciousness of historical distance and difference. But we misunderstand Bécquer's antiquarian interests if we interpret them as a psychological compensation for a penurious life in the early age of mechanical reproduction.[47] Instead, as Rubén Benítez observes, Bécquer's traditionalism bespeaks a sense of historicality unusual in mid-nineteenth-century Spain. In Bécquer, this sense was neither a mystification of the medieval nor history subverted by the present, but History as ruin and rune, as preterite heroic action sustained as intentional object by the poet; that is, history as "palpable" temporality and as "*being*-historical."

Bécquer is often said to have inaugurated modern Spanish poetry; in truth, he did not invent a new poetry for his own time. The problem was that he could find no adequate medium for his exquisite temporal-historical empathy. Neither painting nor Album verse, vaudeville theater or penny journalism, not even "ghost" stories, would suffice. Only in his descriptive essays, modeled on Piferrer and Chateaubriand, and to a lesser degree in his imitations of folk song, could he deploy his anachronistic preromantic sublime. Even in those two modes he was burdened by an excess of the objective signified, in the prose, and by an excess of the subjective signifier, in the poetry.[48] Nor is it proper to speak of a "classic" romantic imagination in connection with Bécquer; for at most what he displays is a rhetorical-hallucinatory sublime. This is shown to best effect in his prose: in the "San Juan de los Reyes" section of the *Historia de los templos de España*, in the *Leyendas*, and in *Cartas desde mi celda*.[49]

European Romanticism in Ruins

Repetition and recollection are the same movement, except in opposite directions, for what is re-collected has been, is repeated backward, whereas genuine repetition is recollected forward. —S. Kierkegaard, *Repetition*[50]

As most specialists would agree, the elucidation of European romanticism is still haunted by the nominalist challenge of Arthur O. Lovejoy's "On the Discrimination of Romanticisms [1924]." Down to the present many critics have taken up Lovejoy's challenge to show that there is one romanticism rather than many. Of these, René Wellek's response is certainly the most enduring. Wellek answered that especially the German, English, and French romantic movements did indeed form a coherent group as to style, theory, and philosophy and that they all held essentially the same conception of the romantic imagination and of man's relationship to nature, as well as a similar use of imagery, symbolism, and myth. Lesser critics have avoided engaging Lovejoy directly by specializing in minor romantics or otherwise circumventing global definition. Nevertheless, because of the work of Wellek, as well as of Earl Wasserman and Meyer Abrams, an enduring consensus on high romanticism was achieved, even though Jerome J. McGann has accused Wellek of "argument-by-exclusion" and J. Hillis Miller and Virgil Nemoianu have chided Abrams for setting up a romanticism that trails away into incoherence.[51]

But concurrently, critics with a redoubtable philosophical training, such as Paul de Man and Jacques Derrida, began, like the Knight in Bergman's *Seventh Seal*, to upset this literary historical chessboard. Thus, Paul de Man concluded a notorious essay with the deconstructive sublimity that "the bases for historical knowledge are not empirical facts but written texts, even if these texts masquerade in the guise of wars or revolutions."[52] In turn, Derrida claimed that metaphysical concepts had caused the "supervening opposition between *physis* and *nomos*, *physis* and *techne*, whose ultimate function [was] perhaps to *derive* historicity."[53] Instead of being constrained by the historization of romanticism, then, de Man and Derrida maneuvered to declare history out-of-bounds. Yet Paul de Man's writings not only contain gnomic definitions of "literature," as in *Blindness and Insight*, but also seemingly historicist definitions of romanticism, as in *The Rhetoric of Romanticism*—for instance, that "the affinity of later poets with Rousseau . . . [is] . . . a valid definition of romanticism as a whole."[54]

After René Wellek, Meyer H. Abrams is the comparatist who has done most to secure the current unified theory of romanticism—definitively, it seemed, in *Natural Supernaturalism* (1971). Centering his work on the "System" Wordsworth expounded in a short *Prospectus* appended to *The Excursion*, Abrams suggested that once the first English romantics became disillusioned with the French Revolution, they internalized the project of making a better world through politics. Thus their poetry became a substitute vehicle for the radical alteration of mankind. Abrams also explained that to structure his autobiography of epic proportions, Wordsworth refashioned the Augustinian psychobiography. Wordsworth poured into a poetic version of the *Confessions* his personal experience of early spiritual illuminations, although now the "grace" for conversion and salvation was provided by Nature, not God. In the *Prospectus*, says Abrams, Wordsworth traced a Way of Perfection; an initial union with Nature, corresponding to childhood and to Genesis; then, a Fall; and finally a redemption, through the Imagination's reeducation by Nature. The process culminated in a "marriage" of imagination and world.

Such was the romantic "plot," which Abrams discovered in Wordsworth's *Prelude*, then in Hölderlin's *Hyperion, or the Hermit in Greece*, and the work of such different writers as Novalis, Hegel, and Rimbaud. Wordsworth's autobiographical conversion scheme described, according to Abrams, a "secular theodicy—a theodicy without an operative *theos*—which retains the form of the ancient reasoning but translates controlling Providence into an immanent teleology." This progression, or "biodicy," according to Abrams, was "a typical romantic *Bildungsgeschichte*."[55] Most extraordinary of all was Wordsworth's notion of an imagination that, once duly sensitized and mentored by nature, developed a force of intellectual love that surpassed its tutor.[56] This secular emplotment by Abrams, or what Nemoianu has reformulated as a penchant for "infinite expansion"—geographic, temporal, societal and mental—offered a coherent, apparently definitive, account of European high romanticism; and it suggested a long life for the ensuing consensus.

Meanwhile, younger critics had begun to give Paul de Man's "Rhetoric of Temporality" careful attention. But so much did its language suggest a continuity with prestructuralist continental phenomenology that de Man was soon forced to speak of the essay as "not only [a change] in terminology and in tone but in substance."[57] The immediate purpose of the essay was not to undo a now virtually canonical romanticism, but to free certain rhetorical figures—allegory and irony—from misunderstandings that dated back to the eighteenth century. Nevertheless, the force of de Man's argument caused a fracture in Johns Hopkins-Cornell-Yale romantic studies, for he also showed that the prevailing understanding of high romanticism was quite flawed.

De Man's antihistorical narrative begins in the late eighteenth century, when "symbol" first begins to edge out other rhetorical terms, including allegory (188). Within English literature, de Man addresses Coleridge's privileging of symbol over allegory. Here he finds a contradictory "description of figural language as translucence . . . in which the distinction between allegory and symbol has become of secondary importance." However, in current poetic and critical practice, based on Coleridge's interpretation, the conception of metaphor and imagery had instead become

> a dialectic between object and subject, in which the experience of the object takes the form of a perception or a sensation. The ultimate intent of the image is not, however, as in Coleridge, translucence, but synthesis, and the mode of this synthesis is defined as "symbolic" by the priority conferred on the initial moment of sensory perception (193).

Wherewith de Man turned to "the main interpretive effort of English and American historians of romanticism," which had focused on the transition from eighteenth-century loco-descriptive poetry to romantic nature poetry. Although productive of criticism, this focus faltered when it attempted to explain how the new nature poetry was different from the earlier loco-descriptive poetry. Most critics thought of the romantic image, de Man says, as reflecting a "relationship between mind and nature, between subject and object"; a relationship that increased in intimacy at the end of the eighteenth century. A problem persisted in even the fine analyses of early romantic poems by Abrams and Wasserman: how to designate a relation between mind and nature that was not simply analogical? The terms usually employed—"affinity," "sympathy"—showed that the notion of the relation with nature had been displaced by an interpersonal one (196).

But—as de Man then pointed out—this contradicted a particular of romantic nature poetry: its "analogical imagination . . . founded on the priority of natural substances over the consciousness of self." In Coleridge and in Wordsworth a confusion appeared over inner and outer, permanence and mutability. Faced with which, Coleridge and other romantic poets, succumbed to the temptation for the self to borrow "the temporal stability that it lacks from nature and to devise strategies by means of which nature is brought down to a human level while still escaping 'the unimaginable touch of time'" (197).

De Man noticed that Wasserman and Abrams were both uncertain about whether romanticism was a "subjective idealism" or a "certain form of naturalism." This confusion, he suggested, arose because the (romantic) poets themselves were "trapped in the contradiction of a pseudo-dialectic between subject and object," and this led later critics incorrectly to suppose that the interpretation of "the romantic image in terms of a subject-object tension" was the main challenge offered by romanticism (198).

Finally, de Man's argument displaced itself laterally to Rousseau and French romanticism. Here de Man returned to the aforementioned *discontinuity* between subject and object: the gardens in *Julie ou la Nouvelle Héloïse* are not symbolic but allegorical, he said. Like Wordsworth's poems dealing with a particular place—Mount Snowdon, the Duddon river—they depend less on specific locale than on "a traditional and inherited typology," to borrow Abrams's phrase.[58] Just like Wordsworth, then, Rousseau rejected the too facile "resources of a symbolic diction" and turned instead to allegory. Because, as de Man says, "allegory always corresponds to the unveiling of an authentically temporal destiny" (206)—a destiny that is quite different from the contingent and spatial world of the symbol, for with allegory

> time is the originary constitutive category. The relationship between the allegorical sign and its meaning (*signifié*) is not decreed by dogma. . . . We have, instead, a relationship between signs in which the reference to their respective meanings has become of secondary importance. But this relationship between signs necessarily contains a constitutive temporal element; it remains necessary, if there is to be allegory, that the allegorical sign refer to another sign that preceded it. The meaning constituted by the allegorical sign can then consist only in the *repeti-*

tion (in the Kierkegaardian sense of the term) of a previous sign with which it can never coincide, since it is of the essence of this previous sign to be pure anteriority (207).

While the symbol makes empty promises of identity, allegory acknowledges a space between itself and its origin and therein establishes its language. In this way it protects the self from any delusional identity with the non-self, specifically with nature. When this delusion is avoided, de Man says, we hear the authentic voice of early romantic literature. But this voice has rarely been understood; instead, romanticism has been taken for a "primitive naturalism" or a "mystified solipsism." In this new perspective, "the dialectic between subject and object" not only ceases to be

> the central statement of romantic thought, but this dialectic is now located entirely in the temporal relationships that exist within a system of allegorical signs. It becomes a conflict between a conception of the self seen in its authentically temporal predicament and a defensive strategy that tries to hide from this negative self-knowledge. On the level of language the asserted superiority of the symbol over allegory, so frequent during the XIXth century, is one of the forms taken by this tenacious self-mystification (208).

To disclose the implications for Wellek's and Abrams's views of romanticism and for postromantic poetry in general, de Man's essay requires a short commentary. De Man declares their interpretations of romanticism inauthentic because they fail to recognize that most romantics sought "refuge against the impact of time in [the] natural world" instead of renouncing the pursuit of ontological stability there, as de Man believes Wordsworth and Rousseau did. Implicit in "The Rhetoric of Temporality," and in "Intentional Structure of the Romantic Image" (1960), is a clear faulting of Abramsian romanticism for having given an incomplete account of an ongoing "dialectic" between consciousness and the ontologically stable natural object.

But then, by precisely what measure is the Wellek-Abrams account incomplete? It helps to know that de Man's criticism of the interpretation

of high romanticism also originates with Hölderlin's chiasmic deployment of the classic-romantic difference, in which each of Schiller's naive
and sentimental poles would describe a movement out to its 'other' or
'foreign', and then, following a renunciation, back to its 'proper' or
'native'. But de Man contends that only the earliest romantics,
Rousseau, Wordsworth, and Hölderlin, actually completed this complex
out-and-back movement. Only they achieved an "authenticity" by
resolving their temporal (and historical) predicament, without succumb-
ing to the Western or "Hesperian" ('foreign') temptation of nature's
ontological stability.

Yet why does de Man's critique also threaten the dissolution of the
"romantic movement" itself? De Man's terminology of "dialectic,"
"inauthenticity," and "temporality," seems to suggest the presence of
Hyppolite, Wahl, and Sartre.[59] But, more to the point, his destabilization of romanticism occurs under the aegis of an innovative "historical
poetics" formulated during the study of Hölderlin's poetry and essays.
Additionally, de Man also participated in the postwar reception of
Heidegger in France.[60] Thus "historical poetics" represents de Man's
understanding of Hölderlin's: "What is lasting is founded by the poets."
With virtually no elaboration he declares that a genuine historical
poetics

> would attempt to think the divide in truly temporal dimensions
> instead of imposing upon it cyclical or eternalist schemata of a
> spatial nature. Poetic consciousness, which emerges from the
> separation, *constitutes* a certain time as the noematic correlate of
> its action. Such a poetics promises nothing except the fact that
> poetic thought will keep on becoming, will continue to ground
> itself in a space beyond its failure.[61]

Only by extension can this "dialectic" be considered Hegelian, even
if influenced to a degree by Schiller's anticipation of Hegel, through the
former's recasting of classic and modern as naive and sentimental.[62]
Instead, it is de Man's extrapolation of Hölderlin's doubling of each term
of Schiller's naive and sentimental pair. At issue, then, is not a dialectic
"of being and non-being, but of immediate presence and [linguistic]
mediation."[63] It was precisely here that de Man took issue with

Heidegger's exegeses of Hölderlin.[64] In contrast to Heidegger's reading, de Man interpreted Hölderlin's "historical poetics" as a poetics of negativity, of the repeated failure to "say" Being. Although Heidegger agreed with Hölderlin on the desirability of "saying" Being (Heidegger: *Wesen*) (Hölderlin: "wunderbar allegegenwartig" [the "wondorously all-present"]), to perceive Nature or Being according to Hölderlin was not to be able to *say* or found it. No sooner is the word spoken than "it destroys the immediate and discovers that instead of stating Being, it can only state mediation."[65] Hence the saving importance for Hölderlin and de Man of poetic mediation and of allegory.

In his exchange with Heidegger we begin to grasp why de Man prefers the fictive temporality of allegory to the feigned spatial simultaneity of the symbol. The former is undeluded as to the inevitability of mediation and can thus be considered authentic, although no existential imperative is intended. Instead, the ethical overtones emanate from the historical concern with the aesthetic education of mankind that Hölderlin shared with Schiller. Yet when Hölderlin developed his peculiar version of classic versus romantic by renaming Schiller's symbolic historical terms, he converted a new, inaccessible classic (a never-existing Greece) and a new romantic (a Hesperia or Germany that was yet to be) into a poetics that bespoke the ultimate truth of all poetry and that, ironically, reversed the subsequent historicization of Schiller's original terms.[66] The result was the "*vaterländische Umkehr*" that Hölderlin developed to enlighten his contemporaries, the Hesperians, and what de Man later termed "historical poetics."

After his work on *Empedocles*, Hölderlin translated or, as he said, "modernized" *Antigone* and *Oedipus Rex*. As his letters and *Notes* on both plays show, he subdivided each side of the classic-modern opposition so that Greece and Europe each potentially acquired a "naive" or 'national' *and* a "sentimental" or 'foreign' pole. Equally original was Hölderlin's notion that since Greece never managed the difficult *Umkehr*, or return to its 'native' (a proto-Nietzschian "sacred pathos") but only attained its 'foreign' (or Homer's "clarity of exposition," which was what Greece was not), it could hardly be a model for "Hesperia" (Germany or Europe) but only an admonition. Consequently, romantic or modern "Hesperia" never completed its "return" either; it too remained its 'foreign' (what it was not). For, as Hölderlin wrote to Böhlendorff, "We learn nothing with more difficulty than to freely use the national."[67] In the end, this was the Hölderlinesque "historical poetics" that de Man used to power "The Temptation of Permanence" (1955), "Process and Poetry" (1956), and "Intentional Structure of the Romantic Image" (1960), the three essays in which he sketched what he called the "postromantic predicament." For what had emerged from Hölderlin's view of the mutual impermeability of classic and modern was a complete *poetic* dialectics of historical becoming. This allowed de Man, in his turn, to assume in his own literary criticism Heidegger's by no means alien notions of "temporality" and "authentic historicality."[68]

In his translations, Hölderlin used the doublet of 'native' and 'foreign' so that his contemporaries would beware of the dangers of taking Greece as a model. If the Greeks were "naturally" mystical and tended to overbalance into the godly realm but had nevertheless at least attained their 'foreign', then Hölderlin's "modernizations" of Sophocles were designed to convey this. That is, they were to show his (Hesperian or Western) contemporaries that their 'native' or 'national' was actually consciousness and clarity, while their 'foreign' was "immediate pathos and sensuousness" (the Greek's *putative* 'native'). Therefore, in Hölderlin's translations of *Antigone*, Zeus became "the father of time," and instead of "watching over the birth of time" Danaë "count[s] the hours" (the time separating her from the natural object). In this oblique manner Hölderlin depicted "un-returned" Hesperian, Western, romantic or modern poets as perennially and mistakenly nostalgic for, even envious of, the ontological stability of natural entities, because they refused to acknowledge their ultimate 'native' or 'national' temporal condition of becoming—or, in Heideggerian terms, their temporality and authentic historicality. Thus, comments de Man, Western postromantic poetry became a mask, a "constant dissimulating through which we attempt to hide from ourselves."[69] In other words, in contrast to Rousseau, Wordsworth, and Hölderlin, late romantic and postromantic poets never managed a 'native' or 'national' return; instead they "fell" into "inauthenticity" among (natural) "world-historical" entities.[70]

Indeed, according to de Man's "Intentional Structure of the Romantic Image," only Rousseau, Wordsworth, and Hölderlin managed a return to the modern's true 'native'—and thus they surpassed even the Greeks. In these three giants the "poetic imagination" succeeded in renouncing nature and moved "upward" toward a non-sensuous realm, imaged by Wordsworth as "Cerulian ether." Returning from their 'foreign', or the ontological envy of nature, to their 'native' or 'national', they directed their longing to "an entity that could never, by its very nature, become a particularized presence."[71] In its turn, this entity—unmediated Being—reminds us of Heidegger's misreading of the "sayability" of the presence of Being or Nature, that de Man pointed out in rereading Hölderlin's poem "Wie wenn am Feiertage. . . ." The nostalgia for, and the renunciation of, natural objects in favor of "the transparency of air,"[72] is simply another aspect of Hölderlin's conceptualization of Becoming and of the poets' subsequent failure to *say* the presence of Being—in its turn a slightly different formulation of the problem of presence and (linguistic) mediation. For both are derived from Hölderlin's proto-Heideggerian idea of history as authentic historicality, according to which the poetic failure to "say" dynamizes a successful ongoing dialectic. For, as de Man writes in "The Temptation of Permanence,"

> In a dialectical movement of the mind, the idea of continuity is no longer essential, for the discontinuity has lost its character of mortal destiny in becoming an integral part of the life of the mind. While the moment of discontinuity is certainly that of death, it is nevertheless also that of renewal, difficult and uncertain, but possible. From this perspective, history is neither passive destiny nor a growth. The only permanence is that intention of the absolute that *creates history*, and the lesson of the past consists in the ["resolute"][73] repetition of this intention, recognized beyond its successive defeats, the remnants of which cover the surface of our earth. The new produces itself by the confrontation of becoming in process with anterior movements, a confrontation through which a unity of intention reveals itself. *The poets seem to have known this more often than the historians.* . . . What the Renaissance drew from the Roman world, or romantic neo-Hellenism from Greece, is not the immediate identity of a permanence . . . but the intention of taking up a prior struggle, with methods that cannot be the same since they have previously failed. The Renaissance nourished itself in meditating, perhaps without knowing it, on the Latin decadence, and it is in

thinking, very consciously this time, the death of Greece that neo-Hellenism produced its major works. Far from being antihistorical, the poetic act (in the general sense that includes all the arts) is the quintessential historical act: that through which we become conscious of the divided character of our being, and consequently of the necessity of fulfilling it, of accomplishing it in time, instead of undergoing it in eternity."[74]

Hölderlin alludes to this "Hegelian" notion of historical change in his essay "Becoming in Dissolution," in reaction to the violence and chaos of the French Revolution. Within the reigning "dissolution," he and his friend Sinclair were able to perceive a model for the coming-to-be of the new and the possible, out of the destruction of the old.[75] Indeed, only *amidst* dissolution could they envision any "becoming." Thus for them, through his recollection and positing, the poet became the foster parent of change. In "Becoming and Dissolution" Hölderlin wrote:

> In the state between being and non-being, however, the possible becomes real everywhere, and the real becomes ideal, and in the free imitation of art this is a frightful yet divine dream. In the perspective of ideal recollection, then, dissolution as a necessity becomes as such the ideal object of the newly developed life, a glance back on the path that had to be taken, from the beginning of dissolution up to that moment when, in the new life, there can occur a recollection of the dissolved and thus, as explanation and union of the gap and the contrast occurring between present and past, there can occur the recollection of dissolution.[76]

There can be no doubt, then, that Hölderlin's "failed"-successful dialectic rewards us with a "completed" reading of the aborted romantic dialectic of subject-object that de Man accused Abrams of abandoning prematurely. Conversely, when he implies, as in "The Rhetoric of Temporality," that romantic poets and their critics are "unreturned," he brings to bear a version of Hölderlin's chiasmic doubling of Schiller's naive and sentimental pair. But de Man's Hölderlinesque "historical poetics" is also constructive: it contains a proposal for a pseudo-historical, or rather a *genuinely* historical ontology of poetry. As we have seen, the early or (pre)romantic titans renounce the inauthentic romantic-modern nostalgia for the ontological stability of natural objects (their 'foreign') and address instead an undefined parousia-like entity, thereby signaling a return to their 'native', their "being-at-home." For both Hölderlin and de Man, Rousseau is the emblematic figure whose meditations on inner tranquillity and measure acquire ontological weight. Although Rousseau's thought no longer focuses on material objects, it lacks no potential for engaging the world. "On the contrary," says de Man, "to the extent that it reestablishes an authentic relation to being, it extends itself to the entire community. . . . Hence it necessarily has an aspect not merely political but revolutionary."[77]

What is certain is that this turn toward an unsayable entity by Rousseau, Wordsworth, and Hölderlin, which signals their autonomy vis-à-vis nature, is not an escape into the beyond. But since this romantic or modern 'native' was scarcely developed by Hölderlin, there is slippage in de Man's delineation of it. Thus de Man's (pre)romantic titans also express their renunciation as a heightened degree of self-consciousness, albeit a "self-consciousness in the form of temporal being"[78] and, even more significantly, as the internalization of Being—as in Wordsworth's case. As we saw earlier, the *high* romanticism that failed to appear in Spain was loosely defined as "the secularization of inherited theological ideas and ways of thinking" (Abrams). Thus, in Protestant countries the internalization first of reason and then, with the romantics, of imagination was an essential ingredient of this secularization. Hence a predisposition for what amounted to the internalization of divinity seems present there, but paradoxically not in "mystical" Spain. This is probably because, as Tillich writes in *History of Christian Thought*, "The subjectivity of Pietism [and] the doctrine of the inner light in Quakerism and other ecstatic movements . . . [have] the character of immediacy or autonomy against the church."[79]

Perhaps now we can comprehend why the "affinity of later poets with Rousseau" so powerfully defines romanticism, why it is precisely *not* historicist, and why, as its present interpreters, Hispanists are also doubly implicated in the study of romanticism. For as we now see, more than the originary messianism of the Jena romantics, or the nested (mis)interpretations of Greece, the true center of romanticism—for critics as for poets—must be this "failed"-successful analeptic interpretation, this (genuine) "historical poetics"—in Spain's case, of its own particularly cathected past. Indeed, the mediation of such interpretations and the meditation on the past are now the only native romantic poetological thought that Spain can have. Therefore it is imperative that we, as Hispanists, turn to Bécquer's interpretive engagement with temporality and historicality as to an authentic "native return," and away from the historical Romantics' and the romantic historians' 'foreign'.

For Bécquer and Hölderlin the past is unrecoverable, and yet its interpretation remains a matter of spiritual life and death. This is why Bécquer's prose and poetry continue to be an enigmatic point of inflection between historical Romanticism and the present, to which generations of poets—and critics—repeatedly return. One poet who explicitly acknowledged this filiation was Luis Cernuda. Therefore, by paying particular attention to his poetic interpretation of this relation, we should be able to discover, beyond historical Romanticism and its national-romantic sequelae, an unremarked variety of "Spanish" high romanticism.

A Restitutional Theory of Spanish Romanticism

The best recent interpretations of Spanish romanticism presuppose a comparative perspective. But even this insurance has not reduced the confusion surrounding the debate. For whenever a romantic author or modality is studied, the discussion is invariably obscured by a poorly focused theoretical frame. Wittgenstein alluded to just this danger when he wrote, "One thinks one is tracing the outline of the thing's nature over and over again, and one is merely tracing round the frame through which we look at it" (*Philosophical Investigations*, #114). This kind of fundamental misperception has reduced comprehension of Spanish romanticism more often than we care to acknowledge.

In fact, descriptions of Spanish romanticism are, with few exceptions, nearly all frame and no picture. This is because, as we have seen, much more is at stake in the question of romanticism than literature. Unless a nation can be said to possess a high romanticism, it does not seem European enough. In keeping with this prejudice, students of

Spanish romanticism have resolved the question in one of four ways: they have either claimed that Spanish literature is innately romantic (E. Allison Peers); they are certain that Spain has never had any romanticism at all (Angel del Río); they take for granted, or go to great lengths to demonstrate, the existence of an early Spanish high romanticism (Russell P. Sebold); or else they allege a late, respectable surrogate, such as Hispanic *modernismo* (Octavio Paz) or the Generation of 1898 (Edmund L. King, Juan Luis Alborg). Finally, it is not by chance that these four positions make two overlapping binary systems: all or nothing, early or late. Thus we must interrogate each cardinal point in turn and then propose a counter-theory to replace all four.[80]

Despite recent efforts by academic critics—especially Russell P. Sebold, Robert Marrast, Donald L. Shaw, Edmund L. King, Susan Kirkpatrick, and David T. Gies—and the poet-critics, Octavio Paz and Guillermo Carnero, it is still unconvincing to speak of outstanding nineteenth-century Spanish writers as high romantics—as is clear on reading the first volume on romanticism in Juan Luis Alborg 's *Historia de la literatura española*.[81] This is because Alborg's account begins with a thorough discussion of recent theory about English and European romanticism, with which he contrasts Spanish romanticism, beginning with the early work of Peers. It was E. Allison Peers who in 1940 relaunched the German romantic idea that Spanish literature was inherently romantic, except, as he said, during the first half of the eighteenth-century when, because of a brief Enlightenment, Spain was not entirely itself. However, once this Enlightenment had past, Spain's inherent conservative romanticism reasserted itself, even though it was also obliged after 1833 to assimilate a foreign romanticism imported by exiles from London and Paris. Peers's second, equally provocative thesis was that this foreign-inspired romanticism soon disappeared into what he dubbed "eclecticism"—a peculiar Spanish compromise between neoclassicism and romanticism that incorporated foreign ingredients compatible with the redoubtable domestic romanticism. It should now be obvious, despite the extravagance of his first thesis, that Peers was far from wrong with his second one.

At first glance the antithesis of Peers's theory sounds equally eccentric. Angel del Río and Donald L. Shaw maintain, with different reservations, that "Spain is the last country that can lay a claim to an indigenous romantic literature."[82] To his credit, Alborg finds this notion as unacceptable as Peers's first thesis. But neither del Río, nor Shaw, nor even Alborg, will admit that there may be no Spanish romanticism at all.

Alborg's own reconstruction of the problem begins with a review of recent work on the Spanish Enlightenment. It could formerly be held, he says, that the weakness (or nonexistence) of Spanish romanticism was caused by a deficient Enlightenment. Now Richard Herr, Russell Sebold, Guillermo Carnero and others have undercut this explanation by insisting on the existence of a not inconsiderable Spanish Enlightenment. Thus, it is no longer reasonable to claim that there was no romanticism because Spain had no Enlightenment to provoke it. In any case, the existence of a Spanish romanticism no longer depends on the return of the exiles. Instead, as Sebold, Carnero, Juretschke, and Flitter have shown, a romanticism appeared on native ground because late neoclassical writers such as Lista—an eclectic in Peers's sense, as we have seen—helped stimulate Espronceda and, indirectly, Bécquer. That is, late Enlightenment figures such as Lista, who proved receptive to preromantic notions, passed these along to their disciples.

In Alborg's view the question of Spanish romanticism should henceforth be approached as follows: examine its gestation in the eighteenth century; in other words, trace its development out of a putative preromanticism. Then, attribute whatever happened in its final major phase (1834–1844) to the vagaries of Spanish political history. Instead of supposing that a weak Enlightenment made a romantic reaction unnecessary, recall that members of the Spanish Enlightenment, many persecuted by absolutism, were subsequently more esteemed in Spain than any European romantics—Byron excepted.

These reflections by Alborg give us a new appreciation of the endurance of Spain's limited Enlightenment. They do not constitute a satisfactory theoretical solution to the problematics of Spanish romanticism. Yet Alborg's special appreciation for Peers's "eclecticism" underlines an embarrassing feature of what presently passes for Spanish high romanticism: its coexistence, or interrelation, with a certain deflated neoclassicism. Peers's two-volume exposition of "eclecticism," then, is actually an acute account of the true literary-historical situation. In point of fact, Alborg wonders, what sort of romantic manifesto could have derived its "rules"—as Alcalá Galiano's Preface to Rivas's *El moro expósito* (1834) did—directly from Luzán's neoclassical *Poética* of 1737?[83] Such a romanticism would perforce be at odds with any genuine high romanticism—especially with M. H. Abrams's paradigm for high romanticism and with René Wellek's mutually implicating romantic thematics. At most one could say that elements of a preromanticism *began* to appear in late eighteenth-century Spain. Yet, despite what Russell Sebold and others aver, this does not guarantee an early, a timely, or even a late, Spanish high romanticism. For preromanticism, as Joaquín Arce remarked, and Marshall Brown confirms, need not issue in a romanticism.

Although to his credit Alborg's reflections have cleared the conceptual air, as a reconstruction of Spanish romanticism, his own contribution is not compelling.[84] Still, since Alborg uses the work of Wellek, Peckham, Wasserman, and Abrams as a benchmark, he must conclude that there is no high romanticism in Spain between 1780 and 1843. His solution to the dilemma is to opt for what he calls a "genuine" romanticism that appears in Spain at the end of the nineteenth-century. There is no question, he says, but that "the complete triumph of romanticism . . . comes with the Spanish disciples of Krause and the Generation of 1898."[85] Thus Alborg seems to subscribe to Edmund L. King's thesis that the best candidate for a Spanish high romanticism is the Generation of 1898—whose members are contemporaries of the Catalán *modernistes* and the Latin American *modernistas*.

Now, to decide the validity of Alborg's proposal, let us put this "late" thesis to the test. However, since the Generation of 1898 is now also under erasure, instead of his or Edmund L. King's version of the thesis, let us select the one Octavio Paz offers in *Los hijos del limo* (1972).[86] According to its subtitle, Paz's book is an account of modern European and American poetry that pays special attention to the Hispanic tradition. In developing the thesis that *modernismo* (1880-1910) is Hispanic romanticism, Paz depicts European romanticism as happening in three successive waves: first there is its creation by German and English romantics; then its metamorphosis into French symbolism and Spanish American *modernismo*; and finally its climax and demise as twentieth-century vanguard poetry. Like Edmund L. King, Octavio Paz rejects the notion of an early Spanish romanticism, but is equally reluctant to do without any romanticism at all.

Paz's own emplotment requires that the notion of romanticism as a reaction to the Enlightenment be retained. He calls Spanish American *modernismo* "a certain romanticism," and then explicates its emergence by stating that Latin American Positivism, in its effects, was a late "equivalent" of the Enlightenment. Although Paz declares that *modernismo* is "our true romanticism," he also later calls it "another romanticism," perhaps in the sense that French symbolism is.[87] Finally, Paz wavers between, on the one hand, acknowledging that there is only an analogical relationship between his three waves of romanticism and, on the other, insisting that since occult philosophy is an invariant in all three, they are substantially the same.

This suggests that the Achilles' heel of Paz's reconstruction is his narrowing of high romanticism to the single ingredient of esoteric analogism, at best a submerged element in Abrams's vastly more complex plot. Indeed, Paz's willful reduction of romanticism—and symbolism—to occultism is perverse. It is impossible not to suspect that in searching for respectable forebears for *modernismo*, he has unfairly reduced European high romanticism's notoriously ample margins.

So much for the contradictory ways in which scholars have framed their conceptions of romanticism. It should be obvious that none of the four cardinal theories will stand by itself. As I have explained, the historical Romanticism that did exist—between 1814 and 1844—became progressively contaminated by politics. This is why instead of employing Juretschke's term exclusively I also reassigned Marrast's "national-romanticism" and Nemoianu's "Biedermeier" to different, successive moments after 1844. But the question then is: If none of the existing theoretical frames is acceptable, what have critics been studying as Spanish romanticism?

My alternative theory entails two related proposals. First, that we acknowledge that what passes for high romanticism—Duque de Rivas, Larra, Espronceda—is a variegated historical Romanticism, and its sequel—Zorrilla, Mesonero Romanos, Campoamor, Fernán Caballero, Bécquer—a "national-romanticism" that develops with certain characteristics that can usefully be labeled Biedermeierish. As Nemoianu says of Mesonero and the other *costumbristas,* "They were chiefly turning back in order to respond to the [foreign] high romantic surge."[88] Thus, jingoistic national-romanticism also assumed a self-congratulatory Biedermeierish cast, which reflected the attitude of "colonial expansionism" that was possible once the final institutionalization of the bourgeois revolution of the 1830s had taken place.[89]

My second proposal concerns the *restitution* of a modern Castilian-Andalusian poetic tradition. Because Octavio Paz seems only to have redescribed *modernismo,* and not to have found our missing Hispanic high romanticism, we still must account for the appearance in Spain of isolated "strong" nineteenth-century romantic poets, and of strong twentieth-century postromantic poets. Although in Spain there was no domestic high romantic *movement,* I maintain that discrete instances of European high romanticism obviously do occur. What took place, then, was a dissemination of the detritus of European high romanticism, either directly or in translation, or indirectly via French symbolism—much in the way explained by Albert Béguin in *L'âme romantique et le rêve: Essai sur le Romantisme allemand et la Poésie française* (1939).

Thus, where "Metropolitan" European countries consumed sizable and "timely" doses of romanticism all at once—or in two successive doses as in France—peripheral Spain (with the other Hispanic countries) received meager and occasional portions of romanticism, the reception of which paradoxically made possible the continuing irruption there of *high* romanticism well into the twentieth century. This restitutional view further suggests that Latin American *modernismo* and Castilian-Andalusian poetry are *parallel* phenomena and that, instead of the former causing the latter, *both* were sparked by European high romanticism, as Octavio Paz indirectly suggests.

With this second proposal the circle closes. As chapter 4 will show, Cernuda's poetry not only fits Abrams's romantic plot as no "Spanish romantic" poetry ever did, but it also illustrates my contention about a Spanish restitutional high romanticism. Therefore, Cernuda's case is no exception; it exemplifies a rule. If, in the nineteenth century, there were José María Heredia's and Espronceda's debts to Ossian, Foscolo, and Lamartine; Larra's, Espronceda's, and Bécquer's debts to Heine; and Bécquer's to Chateaubriand and Heine, then in Spain's extraordinary twentieth century there is Unamuno's debt to Sénancour; Juan Ramón

Jiménez's and Pedro Salinas's debts to Shelley and Keats; Cernuda's debts to Browning, Wordsworth, Hölderlin, and Leopardi; and García Lorca's and Cernuda's debts to Jean Paul Richter. Indeed, the ad hoc restitution of high romanticism also accounts for the unexplained richness of *twentieth-century* Hispanic poetry. *Because* they had not enjoyed local or national high romantic *movements*, Hispanic poets could continue to sift through the ruins of European high romanticism, even after the demise of early European and Anglo-American modernism, and even though by then they were perceived to be speaking vanguard-ese (García Lorca and Neruda, or *Neruda*).[90]

* * *

In the next two chapters I will focus on the prose of Gustavo Adolfo Bécquer (1836-1870) and the poetry of Luis Cernuda (1902-1963) to flesh out this argument. In both essays I treat the aesthetic category of the sublime as a true index of chronology. Despite being written around 1850, Bécquer's prose incorporates a preromantic sublime. By contrast, Luis Cernuda's poetry reveals a postromantic sublime. Thus Bécquer and Cernuda are emblematic of the fate of romanticism in Spain in that Bécquer's prose reflects a national- or Biedermeierish romanticism, while Cernuda's poetry exemplifies the general phenomenon I am expounding: the piecemeal restitution of European high romanticism.[91] Together the fortunes of these poets document the ruin and restitution of high romanticism in Spain—where at no one point did the Castilian-Andalusian poetic tradition concentrate sufficient critical mass to produce a chronological, exclusively high romantic, movement.

CHAPTER III

$\mathcal{B}$écquer $\mathcal{S}$ublime:
$\mathcal{T}$he $\mathcal{P}$rose and $\mathcal{P}$oetry

In this chapter I focus on preromantic aspects of Bécquer's poetics. Once attention is displaced from his "romantic" or "*symboliste*" *Rimas* to his *Historia de los templos de España*, the *Cartas* and *Leyendas*, a more coherent Bécquer emerges. Although twentieth-century poet-critics such as Juan Ramón Jiménez and Jorge Guillén have read Bécquer either as a high romantic or a *symboliste-modernista*, or both, attention to the rhetoric of his prose reveals an eighteenth-century sublime. In other words, in their haste to monumentalize Bécquer, critics have misplaced his originality. For, particularly in the prose, he was clearly neither a high romantic nor a proto-*symboliste* poet, but the proponent of a religiously tinged national-romantic sublime.

Bécquer's National-Romantic Sublime

Thanks to Rubén Benítez and Robert Pageard we now know enough about Bécquer's political and editorial associates to classify him as a *moderado*.[1] In other words, in the political spectrum of the 1860s—which included Carlists, traditionalists and absolutists, Moderates or neo-Catholics (including González Bravo, Valera, and Castelar), O'Donnell's Liberal Union, as well as Progressives and Democrats, Bécquer associated, as editor and friend, with Moderates, that is, with conservative-liberals. This is noteworthy because his conservatism was not only political but cultural. In short, according to Rubén Benítez, there was a "total accord between Bécquer's artistic thought and the tenets of the Moderate Party."[2]

Thus, when Benítez characterizes Bécquer as a *traditionalista* he identifies him as a writer who is a neo-Catholic, whose thought contains a clear Ultramontane strain, and who fits Derek Flitter's designation of Romantic historicism, as well as our own of national-romantic. This includes the belief that Spanish society was originally a perfect creation that had suffered a gradual decline, accelerated, according to Donoso Cortés, by the French Revolution and eighteenth-century Sensism. Benítez shows that Bécquer in his way was as much a traditionalist as Fernán Caballero and that he too was deeply indebted to the thought of Herder and Chateaubriand.

That Bécquer felt a profound sympathy for Chateaubriand's sentimental religiosity is obvious from his first major editorial adventure on arriving in Madrid. This was the famous *Historia de los templos de España* project, which occupied him from 1857 until 1859.[3] Like Chateaubriand he was convinced that a literature whose subject was God and the created world surpassed classical literature in sublimity. In addition to *Le Génie du Christianisme* (1802), Bécquer certainly read *Les Martyrs* (1809), a veritable Christian poetics. And, in his *Historia* project and elsewhere, he repeatedly compared classical ("pagan") art unfavorably with its Christian counterpart. Classical art, for Bécquer as for Chateaubriand, meant harmony of surface detail, indeed a species of perfection. But Christian art surpassed the classical in its represented inwardness, feeling, and pure spirituality. This was why, for both writers, the "sacred remains of Christian monuments" were a favorite object of devout, and by no means melancholy, contemplation.[4]

This makes Bécquer an equally fervent, though considerably more sophisticated, Catholic writer and moralist than Fernán Caballero. Although Bécquer never collected ballads and other popular poetry the way Fernán Caballero did, he nevertheless shared her high estimate of their value as "remnants" of a happier, more harmonious Christian society; this view matched his ultimately Herderian belief that the ways of peasants were inherently "poetic," and that such folk were even likely to create poetry themselves. Nevertheless, like other post–Civil War critics, Benítez also manages to discover a liberal side to Bécquer's character. He finds evidence for this in the sincerity of Bécquer's defense of modernity, and in his occasional references to poverty and social injustice. But one can only say with certainty that Bécquer had admiring friends of every political stripe, that he visited General Narvaez's bedside when the latter was dying, that he had a nodding acquaintance with Juan Valera, that he visited the Spa at Fitero with González Bravo, and that he had close Liberal and anti-Monarchical friends like Narciso Campillo.

In *Bécquer tradicionalista* Benítez explains how Bécquer's "artistic traditionalism" harmonizes with and informs the *Historia de los templos de España,* which was conceived as a series of deluxe illustrated albums on Spanish religious monuments. Although a second volume succumbed to financial problems, as Bécquer's fervor waned, both Rica Brown and Benítez believe that his careful documentation of this planned effort provided an intellectual foundation for the rest of his creative work. As Benítez demonstrates, in addition to using Chateaubriand's pious archaeology as a model, Bécquer shared with Thierry, Michelet, and Carlyle the desire to produce a "true" history that would re-create the spirituality of the past.[5] To implement this historical-prophetic series, Bécquer incorporated multiple perspectives on the monuments of Visigothic, Christian, imperial Toledo. In addition to including a "thinker" (a historian) and an "artist" (or art historian), he also elected to speak in the role of "poet" (or professional prosopopeist). Thus, in one case his goal was to describe the Convent of San Juan de los Reyes: "in its different aspects as a page of history, an imposing monument, and a fountain of poetry, [since it] enjoys the triple privilege of speaking to the intelligence that reasons, the art that studies, to the spirit that creates."[6]

Benítez correctly interprets Bécquer's inclusion of three spokespersons—a historian, an art historian, and a poet—as revealing a desire to convince his readers of the potential *poetic* authority of history. Bécquer was extremely suspicious of what he called "philosophical" or "critical" history. (This use of "critical" to mean destructive of religious belief is an echo of Donoso Cortés and Jaime Balmes.) At best, Bécquer felt, critical history had its uses in the practice of recent history but not where the remote past was concerned. Yet there was even a danger in its success with recent history, for it threatened to destroy the very "tradition" it was investigating. What he called critical history—the "incredulous daughter of our era"—was too skeptical of folk tales and legends. Whereas, from Bécquer's perspective, both these were "invaluable testimonies."[7] This point was crucial because whether documentation were scarce or not, critical history simply blundered ahead, questioning the historical reality of such national heroes as El Cid and Bernardo del Carpio. Thus, to counter the skepticism of this kind of history, Bécquer preferred a poetic perspective. This enthusiasm was what fired his interest in the *Historia de los templos* project. On the one hand, the critical historian with his documents would not leave out any famous names, but he would certainly discount their more fabled aspects. The poetic historian, on the other hand, would focus on just such traditional sources, inasmuch as they were the genuine repositories of Spanish values. The poetic historian would work intuitively with these to reveal the "ideas" that popular tradition attached to these famous names. Thus, for Bécquer as a national-romantic, oral tradition and the ruins of religious monuments were the preferred sources of national values and hence more precious than any historical "truth."[8] Beyond lamenting the abandoned state of nationally significant architectural ruins, bereft in his day of their animating religious ideals, the poet's task was also the "restoration" of their religious aura through the exercise of poetic reconstruction. As Bécquer explains in the sketch "The Royal castle of Olite": "For the dreamer, for the poet, the devastation of time poses no problem; what is fallen, he raises; . . . what is dead, he takes from the tomb and commands to walk, as Christ did with Lazarus" (1068).[9] A better example of the designs of national-romanticism is difficult to imagine.

At the same time, in treating the prose as ancillary to the *Rimas*, critics have too often focused on Bécquer's methodology of recollection and not often enough on his presentation of what he recollects. Apparently, his "thinker" or "professional" historian is charged with refining the ideological component of Spanish history. For as Bécquer says in the introduction to the *Historia*, it is the "thinker" who "resolves the darker problems of history" (830). This means that Bécquer's historian's task is to provide the reader with evidence of the providential nature of historical events such as the Battle of Toro (1476), and Isabel I's assumption of the throne of Castile. Like conservative and liberal romantic historians, then, Bécquer closely follows the *romancero* tradition and accepts the medieval view that the first Arab invasion of Spain was divine punishment for the ancestral crimes of Isabel's ancestors (830). Although once those crimes had been expiated entirely, Spain's efforts were crowned with "the [Christian] capture of Granada, that gigantic poem of eight centuries duration called the Reconquest" (830).

The best description of Bécquer's "historical poetics" is also by Benítez, although this critic is not particularly interested in its political implications. He sees in Bécquer's historical enterprise the workings of a Hegelian poet caught up in the self-revelatory dialectic of the Spirit. In Benítez's words:

> Only the artist can *intuit the ideal truth*. Before a historical site or the ruins that are part of it, any likely detail suffices to produce a curious alchemical reaction. A ray of light, the movement of a shadow, the sound of flowing water, *immediately evokes a world of fantastic imaginings*. Bécquer believes in sympathetic magic: his sensations before the ruins and even *his strangest fantasies coincide with* the ideal truth that the ruins enclose. . . .
>
> He *does not distinguish between intuition and creative fantasy*. At historical sites his sensibility *permits him undefined experiences* productive of literary creation. Historical figures, *wrapped in the mysterious atmosphere of his imagination come alive* as in their own legends. Thus the architect of San Juan de los Reyes, or Cardinal Mendoza, or the medieval statues on their cenotaphs, acquire *a lively reality in his evocations*. . . .
>
> The observer's activity is not autonomous. As an individual he participates in the same organic totality, from which, at some time in the past, the idea separated itself, becoming objectified in the temple or the popular saying. The individual manner of intuitively grasping the idea is predetermined by the unknown power of the total spirit. The *fantasy* is like a *recollection*, it is an almost Platonic reminiscence of the historical memory in vague form in the individual spirit until the momentary *act of communion* [brings it forth]. . . .[10]

The reader will notice, in the italicized passages, various unwarranted assertions. Since for Benítez romanticism and symbolism are epistemologically the same, he is untroubled by the difficulty of distinguishing between the imagined and the perceived in our poet's undertaking. This is one of the dangers in reading Bécquer as a proto-*symboliste* and a modern. But Benítez also assumes for Bécquer the notion, derived from Coleridge, that the imagination has "esemplastic" power. Like most other commentators of Bécquer's poetics, Benítez attributes to him a full-blown high romantic imagination, when the Bécquerian imagination, like that of Lista, is only capable of "recomposing."

A second misstep follows from this basic one: instead of understanding "Bécquer's" presence in his own narratives as the necessary human figure in a sublime landscape, Benítez psychologizes the Bécquerian narrator's experience as telepathy, hallucination, or Platonic reminiscence. Indeed, Benítez's Bécquer "hallucinates" *in* imagination or, failing that, Platonically "recollects" his national past's heroes and events. Thus, for Benitez, Bécquer as historian, becomes the hypersensitive memorialist of his nation's collective historical consciousness. However, while this would logically be the (noncritical) historian's expected role, it was not the one Bécquer chose for his Poet in the *Historia*.

Benítez's view of the romantic imagination is distorted by the critical "frame" of an (uncompleted) high romantic dialectic between mind and nature. This is of course inappropriate in Bécquer's case, for nature in his poetry is picturesque setting or Platonic topos. Thus no such "natural" romantic exchange could ever take place. What is more, the active "collective" memory of past history that Benítez has Bécquer share is simply not in the text, especially not when the Poet's voice is activated.

In a similar vein, Benítez misinterprets Bécquer's references to the new science of archaeology, to the deciphering of hieroglyphics and the interpretation of Masonic symbols. For although he correctly links Kabbalistic codes to romanticism, Benítez errs in believing that in Bécquer satisfactory "communication" is possible between past and present, or between earth and heaven. Thus he implies that, in calling the Masonic symbols a "forêt de symboles," they are ultimately readable, whereas Bécquer's contention is that they are undecipherable. What "act of communion," then, does pertain between the poet and his historical site?

Contradicting Benítez's view, Bécquer hints that communion with the spirit of the past is at best problematic. In a visit to this same ruined Convent of San Juan de los Reyes described in the fourth of his *Cartas literarias a una mujer*, Bécquer as narrator, identifiable by his dreaminess and sketch book, clearly states that he has only "imagined" the fantastic happenings described: "My longings began to boil and to rise in a steam of fantasy" (681). He further states that the "ideal figure" that he

"seemed to see" is really a statue fallen off its pedestal, leaning in a cor-
ner of the darkened cloister. What he beheld, then, was simply a random
collection of statues, "an entire generation of granite, silent and motion-
less. . ." (681). This moves him to say, in a gesture that will be repeated
by Cernuda:

> Here we have . . . a world of stone; inanimate phantoms of other
> beings that existed, and whose memory is a legacy to future
> epochs of a century of enthusiasm and faith. Solitary virgins,
> austere cenobites, brave martyrs who, like me, lived without
> loves or pleasures; who, like me, eked out an obscure, miserable
> existence, alone with their thoughts and an ardent, inactive
> heart beneath a tunic, like an entombed corpse (682).

These same lifeless statues also provide Bécquer with an opportunity
to invoke their emblematically empty and sightless eyes. Because the
presences turn out to be statues, their pupils are "without light."
Nevertheless, he says, their eyes are raised to heaven, "as though the
sculptor wanted to show that their gazes were lost in the infinite in
search of God" (683). While in this vignette the status of the statues is
perhaps ambiguous, the infinity of their gaze is not: the sightlessness of
the statues strongly implies the distance of the Godhead. The most
starkly negative version of this eye code is in Bécquer's savage story,
"Faith Saves," in which an icon of the Virgin accepts the promise of one
sister's emerald-green eyes as pledge or "ex voto" in exchange for revers-
ing a mysterious illness that afflicts the other sister, which leaves the
donor-sister totally blind.

In support of his point about successful communication with the
past, Benítez conflates different, as well as differently cast, writings.
Together with art-historical segments from the "San Juan de los Reyes"
part of the *Historia*, he combines loco-descriptive passages of a second
visit to San Juan de los Reyes that Bécquer recorded in *Cartas literarias a
una mujer* (letter 4). Neither one supports his point. In the loco-descriptive sequence about earth-bound statues from the *Cartas literarias*,
Bécquer's text implies incommunication and not what Benítez (and
other critics) wishes to show. Instead, in the art-historical segments from
the San Juan de los Reyes part of the *Historia*, we are offered an unusually

vivid example of what can henceforth be called Bécquer's national-romantic sublime. As I shall explain, Bécquer's evocations are not to be construed as simple communications from, or historical reconstructions of, the past, but as "resolute repetitions" on the order of the Heideggerian "conversation with the past."[11]

Bécquer's Preromantic Sublime

"O les belles, les sublimes ruines!"
—Diderot[12]

Why the pronounced antiquarian interest in Bécquer? The poetic modality of the *Historia* is never elegiac but instead hovers between solemnity and the captation of a national-romantic sublimity. Bécquer shows no interest in the picturesque for its own sake,[13] nor does he simply dwell on the baleful spectacle of ruin like the Count de Volnay. Bécquer does not neglect the sociological correlation between Toledo's abandoned churches and the decline of faith. In addition to the ruin of time and the devastation caused by the War of Independence and the Carlist wars, he clamors against official administrative neglect, which he sees as unfortunately consonant with the contemporary decline in religious belief. For this reason, the politically conservative purpose of the *Historia* was to celebrate, and to invite meditation on, the spiritual force of the high points of Spain's national-Catholic past: such as the union of Castile and Aragon through royal marriage, the Reconquest, and Columbus's discovery of America.[14]

As Bécquer recalls in the fourth of his *Cartas desde mi celda*, he had dreamed as a callow youth in Seville of winning eternal fame either as a Christian knight or as a "divine" poet like Herrera. These early dreams seem to have crystallized in the "great poem" of the *Historia* project. Bécquer's object was to provide the images, and the "composition of place," for a series of national "spiritual exercises." However, he must have realized that his use of the eighteenth-century meditation on ruins tended to undermine his purpose, and hence his eventual disillusionment with the project. For in showing that Christian ruins were indices of *past* glory, what he really drew attention to was that although they might be portentous signs they were still ruins, as well as runes in need of an interpreter. Then why did Bécquer invest so much of his health and financial resources in this effort of epic proportions? For it nearly became the inscriptionless funeral monument he proleptically imagined for himself beside the River *Betis* in Seville. A deeper artistic satisfaction must have been involved, beyond such adolescent dreams of personal renown.

Based on Bécquer's literary-archaeological essays, Ramírez Araújo has also formulated an argument regarding Bécquer's reconstruction of the past. The poet's fantasy recomposes the ruined remnants ("vestigios") around an original ideal matrix that he somehow intuits or posits. This parallels what Benítez's "traditionalist Bécquer" does. Indeed, in the fourth of the *Cartas desde mi celda* Bécquer does prefer the Poet's "moral science" of the past to history and archaeology. The former is essential to any national well-being, for "What is left of our absolute [imperial] dominion but a shadow of what was?" (581). Moreover, Bécquer says, if national history is *only* accessible through history and archaeology, then one's reaction must be "disdainful pity." For without their deeper motivations Spain's national heroes will appear as motivationless as marionettes (584).

According to Bécquer, Spanish national life requires the restoration of its past ideals. Because nothing that is present provides a basis for his "lofty speculations," some surviving fragment is needed to support a *hypothetical* reconstruction of the past. But notice that in the fourth of the *Cartas desde mi celda*, to which both Benítez and Ramírez Araújo refer, Bécquer speaks alternately as speculative moral philosopher and as poet. Still, both critics mix these two voices in a composite poetics that they attribute to Bécquer. However, it is crucial to distinguish between the voices. In the same fourth *carta* Bécquer says

> I believe in the future. I am pleased to share mentally in that immense and irresistible invasion of new ideas that is slowly transforming the face of Humanity. . . . Nevertheless, whether for its poetry, or because it is inherent in the fragile nature of man to sympathize with what perishes and to look back with sad complacency at what is no more, in truth, in the depths of my soul, I have consecrated a kind of religion to, I have a profound veneration for, whatever belongs to the past; and the poetic traditions, the ruined fortresses, the ancient customs of our Old

Spain, all have for me that indefinable enchantment, that vague
mystery of the sunset after a day of splendor, the hours of which,
filled with emotions, return in memory again, dressed in colors
and light, before they are buried in that darkness where they
will be lost forever (579–580).

This is the voice of Bécquer the "moral philosopher" acknowledging
the discontinuity of past and present. In contrast the failure to arrest
events causes Bécquer the "poet" a special frisson *because* they fall inex-
orably into the abyss of time, and are reexperienced as the afterglow of
the past, indicated by his use of vivid descriptive hypotyposis. Together
with the figure of personification, the latter is Bécquer's preferred rhetorical device for evoking the national-romantic sublime. Just as in
Espronceda's ode "Al sol," where the sun, even as it "sets," is sublime in
its magnitude—like the imperial past—in contrast to the fallen present.
Through these evocations the "poet" re-experiences the hours that are
past, which "flare up" and are the more precious, like the final blaze of
sunset. It is this "resolute" poetic dialogue that Benítez and Ramírez
Araújo term the successful reconstruction of the past, and would designate as Bécquer's poetics of history.

However, once we set aside a proto-*symboliste* view of Bécquer, a different contextualization of his historical poetics imposes itself; one that
even extends to the *Rimas*.[15] For Bécquer studied poetry and rhetoric
with Rodríguez Zapata, who was a disciple of the neoclassical teacher-
clergyman turned historical Romantic, Alberto Lista. The teacher of
Bécquer's teacher, and an adept of Hugh Blair's *Lessons of Rhetoric,* as we
saw, Lista was as widely known for his political and literary journalism as
for his Ateneo courses on Spanish literature.[16] Thus, instead of simply
asserting the modernity of Bécquer's poetics, it is more instructive to
review his rhetorical practice in the light of Lista's Ateneo courses and
his essays on poetry and rhetoric.

That Bécquer followed Lista's Blair-inspired precepts is clear from his
extensive use, especially in the prose, of personification. For Bécquer and
Lista personification is essential in the articulation of the sublime. But
Bécquer's use of rhetoric is naturally not restricted to his prose; it also
appears in the poetry, a fact scarcely noticed until now.[17] As Benítez
remarks, "The descriptive techniques of artistic traditionalism are easiest

to see in the *Historia*, but they persist in the rest of Bécquer's works; not only in his [assorted] articles on monuments but also in the *Leyendas* and the *Rimas*."[18] Of particular note, given the supposedly biographical nature of Bécquer's poems, is the fact that while his prose abounds in what Lista termed figures of *passion*, his poetry contains instead figures of *reason* and of *expression*, directed primarily at the intellect. As defined by Lista, figures of reason are those "applied to thought when the mind,[19] freed of passion, would demonstrate a truth and expound it with as much clarity and energy as possible."[20]

Before we examine Bécquer's rhetoric of personification in the *Historia de los templos de España*, we should recall the anachronism that this figure of speech represented in 1857. For instance, in drafts of *The Prelude*, written fifty years before, Wordsworth avoids personification when he retrospectively evokes the suggestive presences that visited him in childhood. At first, Geoffrey Hartman says, he may apostrophize these "modes of the other" or use the myth of the *genius loci*, because "that kind of personification is ancient, allows the vocative, and does not merge being into beings."[21] But, continues Hartman, "The later, more complete transformation of such genii into an entirely humanized perception is one of Wordsworth's achievements." Bécquer, coming much later, uses personification unself-consciously; nor, as the episode with the statues shows, was he usually visited by *natural* presences. Rather, in the *Historia* at least, his uncanny experiences occurred with historical characters. However, what Bécquer does share with Wordsworth and other poets of the sublime is the double poetic perspective on such experiences: the lyric "I" must have both a "direct" experience of, and also be able to meditate retrospectively—and proleptically—on, the sublime event. Thematically closer still to Bécquer would be Thomas Warton, who preferred to brood on Stonehenge because, like Bécquer's gothic convent, it was a national rather than a classical monument.[22]

Once Boileau's translation of Longinus's *Peri Hupsous*, Thomson's *Seasons*, Young's *Night Thoughts*, and translations of Milton's *Paradise Lost* became available, Spanish poets were in a position to practice a poetry of the natural sublime. But while in England the sublime easily evolved away from the religious sublime of Addison, Dennis, and Lowth to the late romantic sublime of Hazlit and Keats, in Spain it long retained its "primitive" religious, eighteenth-century cast. In England, as the sublime became less a religious or even supernatural experience, it was replaced as poetic fulcrum by the imagination. But since as late as 1840 the poetic epistemology of Espronceda had scarcely caught up with Thomson, not much more could be expected of Bécquer.[23] In fact, nothing makes Bécquer's preromanticism so evident as his vagueness regarding the viability of the imagination. It seems he was scarcely in advance of Addison, who in *The Pleasures of the Imagination*, chapter 7, recommended personification as a function of the otherwise passive imagination, or as a kind of external, objective "Imagination." That Bécquer had no qualms about employing this figure is clear from the opening pages of the *Historia*. Once we are placed on guard, Bécquer's Introduction to "San Juan de los Reyes" is clear in this respect. He begins:

> Religious tradition is the diamond axis on which our Past turns.
>
> To study temples, the visible manifestation of the former, so as to create a synthesis of the latter in a single volume: that is our intent.
>
> To this end, we shall evoke from the forgotten tombs where they sleep at the foot of the sanctuary, those titans of art who erected it.
>
> They will tell us how the Cross emerged from the catacombs to post itself on the altar to Jupiter, and why since the old form could not contain the new ideas, the latter conceived a special architecture which, migrating from nation to nation, changed through the ages.
>
> From their lips we shall learn what mysterious transformations. . . .
>
> . . . .
>
> Last, when the arts have revealed their secrets . . . we will cast over the confusing chaos of these different ideas a ray of the faith that created them, and this will be the *Fiat Lux* that will dissipate the shadows of this unknown past.
>
> . . . .
>
> Perhaps when, with its fragments fitted together, we stand the Colossus of belief again on its feet, its gigantic proportions will humble and confound the sickly Babel of impiety (827–828).

Inasmuch as "to evoke" means to call forth spirits or the dead by magic charm, it could be said that the whole project of the *Historia*[24] turns on a powerful and overarching prosopopeia of which the Poet's contribution is the most important. While the work of the feigned collaborating artists, historians, and archaeologists forms a theatrical backdrop, it is the Poet who performs the literal rite of evocation.

In his re-creation of the ruined Convent of San Juan de los Reyes, Bécquer chose a four-part format. After giving the historical account of why Isabel I was moved to found San Juan de los Reyes, as well as the art-historical description of its dilapidated remains, Bécquer completed his treatment with a sustained apostrophe to the building's physical ruins, and with a "lyrical" Coda—which forms the fourth part. As is the custom, in order to increase the grandeur of the sublime experience, the poet insists on the inadequacy of language. But since this tends to undermine the purpose of the *Historia*, Bécquer also asks the convent ruins for inspiration. The poet's wish is not for greater eloquence but for help in animating the inanimate and in making the invisible visible; that is, assistance in his visionary-rhetorical enterprise. For the Poet must give a "face" to the spirit of "national-Catholicism" that prompted the original construction of San Juan de los Reyes.

However, since the "natural" sublime, like the national-romantic sublime, presupposes a "real" prior experience, Bécquer—as poet—depicts himself as enthralled by his sublime object—in this case, the actual ruins of San Juan de los Reyes in Toledo. This helps increase the theatricality of the Poet's coda (part 4) where, far from indulging, as Benítez says, in "arrebatos líricos" ("lyrical expostulations"), [25] Bécquer unself-consciously employs descriptive hypotyposis. As Longinus noted, "The Imagination is so warm'd and affected, that you seem to behold yourself the very things you are describing, and to display them to the life before the Eyes of an Audience." And, as Angela Leighton remarks, "What the hand has written is translated back to what the imaginative eye first sees. Communicating to others in words is thus not intrinsic to the act of creation, but is a kind of fallen and generous attempt to repeat the original vision."[26]

In point of fact, Bécquer's description includes the three classic stages of the natural or Kantian sublime: first, an initial untroubled communion of mind and object; then a point of "blockage," in which the object overwhelms the mind's capacity to absorb its magnitude or significance, also called the point of "subreption" (Kant's term); and a final third stage in which the subject grasps its own superiority to the object, either by providing rational support for the over-extended imagination, or, as in romantic art, by "introducing a human scale of measurement into the representation—a human figure into the landscape, or a human motive into the natural history."[27]In "San Juan de los Reyes" the first stage of the sublime is of course the apostrophe: "Bathe my forehead with your peaceful shadows . . ."; the second stage—the moment of blockage—is indicated by these words: ". . . absorbed, vague imagination drifts from marvel to marvel, and unable to encompass all that strikes my eyes, it is dazzled, overwhelmed, offering up an homage of stupefaction to so much grandeur"; and the last stage, which saves the mind from Wordsworth's "abyss of idealism," is indicated by the poet reactively troping the experience of the object through personification: "When I personify the sentiment you [ruins] cause me, I seem to see. . ." (897–898).

The complete Coda or part 4 of "San Juan de los Reyes" is then an extended nine-section descriptive hypotyposis, with each new section indicating a different focus of the original apostrophe. Thus, section 1 begins: "Silent ruins of prodigious art . . . here I am before you. Hail, companions of meditation and melancholy, hail. I am the poet" (897). Instead of "reducing [the ruins'] majesty to a draughtman's drawing, or its "memories to numbers," Bécquer asks for asylum, for a ray of inspiration, for peace and, like a poet of sensibility, begs that the (personified) "melancholy asleep in your breast wrap me in its transparent wings."[28] Now we understand why figures of passion are apposite here in the prose. Lista taught that as opposed to the logic of understanding—which deals with ideas and judgments, or with imagination, which brings thought as near as possible to the senses—the logic of the passions shows man "the objects most likely to excite [the latter]." Here Lista, following Hugh Blair, especially recommends figures like "exclamation," "query," "hyperbole," "apostrophe," "personification" and "vision" or "illusion."[29]

Section 2—of part 4—opens with the words, "At last my steps tread your mysterious sanctum; absorbed, vague imagination strays from one marvel to another, and unable to encompass all that strikes [its] eyes, it is dazzled, overwhelmed," and so forth. This is where Bécquer himself uses the rhetorical term *personification*: "When I personify the sensation you

[O Ruins] cause me, I seem to see among you a monk whose thrown-back cowl reveals brows banded by a warrior's helm, while beneath his religious habit bright chain mail can be seen. . ." (898). Then the personification is effected. Since the notion Bécquer wishes to embody of the founding of San Juan de los Reyes is "mystical and chivalric," the warrior-monk who seems to materialize and cross the sanctuary is an apposite rhetorical hypotyposis.

Section 3 further animates the ruins: they are "children of the faith of a warrior and of a saint" and, what is more, are of noble lineage. This section consists of a vivid evocation of the final moments of the victorious Battle of Toro. In section 4 the original architect of San Juan de los Reyes materializes; so this section is properly a prosopopeia, because the anonymous figure at his desk "ponders" as well as speaks. In section 5 Bécquer avoids taxing his readers' patience by having "the years condense" so as to show the finished convent, lulled by the melancholy music of the Tagus River. King Boabdil, the Moorish enemy to the South, succumbs, and the completed convent is festooned with trophies brought back from the conquest of Granada, offered, Bécquer says coyly, by the *first* Isabel of Castile.[30] Then Columbus discovers America, while the convent "looks on" approvingly.

But Bécquer must acknowledge that time and barbaric humanity "have erased from your visage all signs of those days of pomp and rejoicing. [Now] only one power can momentarily restore your lost beauty and splendor: the power of the enthusiastic mind of the poet" (901). Section 6 climaxes with the now less urgent demonstration of this power; Bécquer's invention "reanimates" the original ruined convent before our eyes; that is, the declarative sequence of first-person verbs "I see," "I feel," "I watch" and (I) hear recreates rather than describes the referent. Thus, when Bécquer writes "I see . . . stained-glass windows cover the broken Gothic arched windows," we understand that it is happening "now."[31] If we fail to see this, the poet has at least put us on notice regarding his sentimental participation in a spectacle of instantaneous re-creation. The vivid description of armor, battle, sunset, and architectural construction suggests that for Bécquer the convent (which he now stands before, now within) is an environment that he not only feels, but that surrounds and penetrates him to such an extent that he becomes its medium.[32]

Now the decline begins. In an autumnal convent scene, Cardinal Cisneros, as a young Galahad-priest, is brought briefly to life. Then, in a curious anachronism, Bécquer chides the knights buried in the convent for not rising to defend it from future (but to Bécquer, past) desecrations. Of these the latest ignominy is the convent's occupation by French troops. Its use as a garrison headquarters and stables by the French, as Bécquer "envisions" it, was climaxed by an apocalyptic arson, the description of which covers a page and a half. Interspersed with first-person exclamations, Bécquer depicts a Dantesque scene of billowing smoke, blue and yellow tongues of flame, even boiling lava. However, the only "mortal" victims are the reanimated statues that stoically see themselves burn. The conflagration is particularly remarkable for its effect on Bécquer, as extra-intra-diegetic narrator-observer. The personified and anthropomorphized dome over the convent church transcept collapses, codexes scatter, the poet warns us (and himself?) "Back! Back!" and we learn that: "[his and our] eyes have been momentarily blinded, [by] a cloud of hot ash and thick smoke (from the collapsing dome) [that] covers this horrible picture ["cuadro"] with a funeral pall."[33] A final episode—which is anticlimactic—seems to imitate Chateaubriand. A benevolent, restorative nature has overgrown the collapsed convent ruins, as though to compensate for their ruination by the twin destroyers, time and mankind.

Ironically, Bécquer's vast *Historia* project itself has only survived as a sublime ruin. He was forced to abandon it because of health and financial problems and to abandon his adolescent dream of creating a "magnificent poem," as his friend Julio Nombela informs us. But at least in the extended Coda to "San Juan de los Reyes" we possess a prose outline of what was to be Bécquer's national-romantic epic.

In the *Historia* Bécquer is concerned with a rhetorically effective translation of sublime experience. This, as described by Lista, was any experience in which one senses "the workings of a superior power" ("un gran poder puesto en ejercicio").[34] For Lista the sublime was only an increment of beauty, never its opposite. And thus, since sublimity for Lista was religious, moral beauty and the sublime were never in disharmony. According to Lista, this "idea of a power, which is what moves and elevates our souls, does not interfere with an object's harmonious relations with the physical and moral order of the universe." Finally,

Lista followed Blair in agreeing that an adequate rhetoric of the sublime employs such figures of passion as personification, apostrophe, and vision.[35]

Although Bécquer's sublime was just as religious as Lista's, he took greater pains to distinguish between the beautiful and the sublime. For Bécquer, too, beauty meant harmony and symmetry, but the sublime, with its aura of a higher power, was other than the beautiful. For example, in the ninth of the *Cartas desde mi celda*, which centers on the report of a legend about the Virgin of Veruela, Bécquer contrasts painting the beautiful with imagining or speaking of the sublime. In this legend of how a church dedicated to the Virgin of Veruela came to be built, Pedro Atarés, a hunter trapped in a terrible storm, prays to the Virgin and sees her descend to earth. Later, he honors her request for a church where she alighted. Bécquer observes, "I would like to have the strength of imagination to 'figure' ("figurar") what it was like" (652).

To illustrate the advantages of imagining over both writing and painting, he compares this legend with Murillo's great paintings of "mystical scenes" and "saintly visions." While Murillo in his paintings may attempt to capture "a ray of that diaphanous atmosphere in which angels swim as in an ocean of luminous vapor," the painter is hobbled by having to use "claroscuro," both light *and* dark, to convey the desired "explosion of clarity." Although, according to Bécquer, we are initially struck by Murillo's canvases, we soon realize that he is "struggling with limited means [to convey] the idea of the impossible" (652). Thus, like "San Juan de los Reyes," the provincial Sorian legend of Pedro Atarés contains an instance of the sublime, inasmuch as it displays a decidedly supernatural personification—actually an epiphany. We are to understand that the discursive freedom of the legend succeeds where Murillo's painting does not: Bécquer, as narrator, in his imagined participation, can imagine or describe contrasting intensities of sublime light that are impossible to paint. According to Bécquer, what "cannot be said with words or translated by sounds or colors" can at least be imagined as "a vivid brilliant splendor surrounding, brightening everything: . . . that compenetrates object[s], making them seem like glass, and at its main point of radiation . . . [is] a light within the light" (652). This rhetorical dilemma is solved in this *carta* by "imagining" light within light, contrast without difference. Bécquer writes:

Finally, I imagine all the splendors of heaven and earth joined in
a single harmony, and in the middle of that source of light and
sound, the Celestial Lady, shining as one flame shines more
brightly than all the others on a hearth, as another more brilliant sun shines within our sun (653).

Desdemona's Handkerchief

Muchas de las rimas de Bécquer, ¿qué son sino peteneras, soleares,
malagueñas, sevillanas mayores?
—Juan Ramón Jiménez[36]

Let us now turn to the poetics of the *Rimas* for further examples of
the Becquerian sublime. Here we anticipate a different rhetoric than in
the *Historia*. Yet it contradicts received wisdom to learn that Bécquer's
poetry uses figures of reason, while his prose employs figures of passion.
For the critical nostrum is that Bécquer's poetry epitomizes spontaneity
and sentimental expressiveness. Yet Carlos Bousoño demonstrated forty
years ago that the spontaneousness of the *Rimas* is only apparent.
Indeed, the discovery of Bécquer's use of opposite rhetorics in the prose
and the poetry only confirms Bousoño's demonstration of the *Rimas*'s
premeditated complexity.[37] But while in the *Rimas* this rhetoricity takes
its phrasing from the German *lieder,* it owes its ultimate sublimity to the
presence of *cante jondo* (deep song). Of course, this popular affiliation is
a Herderian trait Bécquer shares with early historical Romantics like
Böhl, Lista, and Durán.

To date critics have said little about Bécquer's poetry and the sublime. Indeed, by focusing on the poetry rather than the prose, they have
made the exegesis of both considerably more difficult. In his prose
Bécquer moved easily between narration and description, primary
modalities of the secular sublime for all the great romantic prose writers.
But it was one thing to imitate Chateaubriand's descriptions of sublimely
ruined religious monuments in the *Historia* and quite another to invent a
short sublime lyric. Moreover, as Bécquer intimated in comparing painting and imagining, the sublime, especially in its religious variety, was virtually impossible to represent. The formal problem that he confronted,
then, was to discover an adequate poetic vehicle for a more secular sub-

lime. Although Madrid literary circles enjoyed translations of German ballads and *lieder*, Bécquer sought his sublimity in the same Andalusian *cante jondo* that inspired Alberto Lista and Augusto Ferrán.[38] As a national-romantic, Bécquer believed the most likely vehicle for the sublime was folk poetry, of which, as a Sevillano and amateur folklorist, he also had extensive knowledge. According to Bécquer's niece, Julia, both Gustavo and Valeriano played the guitar and sang Andalusian folk songs to entertain their children. Thus, following Ferrán's lead, Bécquer inaugurated the singular practice, followed by modern Spanish poets, of delegating responsibility for a secularized sublime to popular—usually Andalusian—poetry.

In examining Bécquer's poetry, we must also keep in mind that there was no native poetic epistemological tradition to generate the aesthetico-psychological category of the poetic imagination. As I have suggested, Spain completely missed the major legacy of romanticism to modern Anglo-American poetry: that is, an abiding "concern with the situation and process of individual consciousness, and the expression of consciousness in works of imagination."[39] So that, to the extent Bécquer followed Lista's ideas in his poetry, his conception of the sublime remained rhetorical or uncanny. In "San Juan de los Reyes," part 4, Bécquer's sublime typically involved the virtual subsumption of the Poet *into* the figure of descriptive hypotyposis, expressive of his national-romantic, quasi-religious, awe. Of course, this quasi-religious attitude in the prose, and his unself-conscious use of personification, were precisely what made Bécquer's sublime anachronistically eighteenth-century.[40] Yet in the absence of a romantic imagination, personification was the only means at Bécquer's disposal for projecting his "imagined" national heroes. Now let us turn to the virtual secularization of the sublime in the *Rimas* (1870).

In the most complete modern exposition of the influences on his poetry, José Pedro Díaz shows that Bécquer was one of many poets who modeled their work on two primary sources: translations of German art-folk lyrics and Andalusian folk poetry. He also shows that critical awareness of this fact dates back to a decade after Bécquer's death, when the novelist Emilia Pardo Bazán published "The Spanish Fortunes of Heine" in the *Revista de España* in 1886. She pointed out that José María Dacarrete had preceded Bécquer, specifically in imitating Heine.[41]

Later, Juan Ramón Jiménez, not usually so even-handed, also pointed out that in Augusto Ferrán's *La Soledad* (1861) "the blondest of German popular Muses had married the darkest of popular Andalusian 'cantaores,'" but that in distilling this blend, Bécquer had surpassed Ferrán. Of course, Vicente Barrantes (1829–1898) had already observed in the Preface to his Neo-traditional *Baladas Españolas* (1854) that "popular" poetry was the very lyrico-narrative *bonne à tout faire* that Spanish romantics had been looking for. The ballad, said Barrantes, had "the simplicity of the eclogue, the warmth of legend, the melancholy of the traditional ballad, and the sprightliness of folk songs."[42] Thus, in his search for a poetic site for the sublime, Bécquer had only to follow the indications of Blair and Lista. Their prescription for the sublime consisted of these requirements: that it be cast in a short form; that its allusions be circumscribed; and that it be plain, direct, and unadorned.[43] When we combine this with Bécquer's national-romanticism, or "traditionalism" (as Benítez put it), it is clear why Ferrán's *La Soledad* impressed him so.

In fact Bécquer had first used Andalusian folk song in the poetry he wrote for the theater, beginning with *La novia y el pantalón* in 1856, or one year after his neoclassical-allegorical "Ode to Quintana." Thus, while the first Bécquerian *Rimas* date from about 1859–1860, there is reason to suppose that Bécquer was not behind Ferrán and Dacarrete in appreciating Andalusian folk songs, especially the "soledad" or "soleá" and the "seguidilla gitana," by then garnering international fame as flamenco or "Cante flamenco."[44]

Although misinformed about its origins, Bécquer assimilated the Andalusian *cante jondo* to his national-romantic perspective; if the ruins of Toledo compressed millennia of Christianity, in Bécquer's view the "surviving" "Gypsy *cante jondo*" represented a different survival. As he wrote in "La feria de Sevilla," following a late night celebration the Gypsies could be heard in the distance, sadly singing and clapping time. They seemed an ancient, racially pure people, "ecstatic and serious like the priests of an abolished cult who meet in the dead of night to recall glories of former days and to sing tearfully, like the Jews *super fluminem Babiloniae* [sic]" (1289).[45] Bécquer's "costumbrista" message was that today the Gypsies' Babylonian captor is industrialization and that although progress may delight the philosopher, destruction of folklore is a loss to the painter and the poet.

A careful reading of Bécquer's review of Ferrán's *La Soledad* (1861) shows that the latter's poetry fell short of the ideal of the best Andalusian *cante jondo* (or of the current syncretic ideal based on German *lieder* and *cante jondo*). Indeed, although Bécquer alleges lack of space in his review, the sixteen "cantares" by Ferrán he does quote are certainly the best: the remaining 160 folk songs in *La Soledad* are, with few exceptions, devoid of sublimity. On the other hand, as Bécquer's review makes clear, the four-verse *cante jondo* was the perfect antidote to the Esproncedan sublime. If, as Lista remarked, Lope de Vega's *Corona Trágica* was a long poem with one sublime verse in it, it was better to write a sublime poem one verse long.[46] Although published in November 1862, Bécquer's vignette "La Venta de los Gatos" confirms this fascination with *cante jondo*. The prose sketch is set in a popular Andalusian tavern like those that his brother Valeriano painted. Its plot is that of a tragic love story complicated by unemployment, and it incorporates two examples of four-verse, octosyllabic *cante jondo*, the second of which is chillingly sublime. What is interesting about this example is that both Ferrán and Bécquer imitated it, and we can compare their expertise at reworking Andalusian folk song. Clearly, in the gruesome detail of the beloved's hand hanging from the municipal death wagon, Bécquer saw an Andalusian equivalent of the disproportionately great sublime effect achieved by Shakespeare with Desdemona's handkerchief. In Bécquer's version the soleá reads:

> En el carro de los muertos
> ha pasado por aquí,
> llevaba la mano fuera,
> por ella la conocí.[47]

> In the [municipal] death wagon
> "X" passed me by,
> with that one hand hanging out
> I knew it was she.

If we compare Bécquer's famous Rima I, probably written about this time, with his *La Soledad* review, there is further confirmation that Bécquer saw the Andalusian *cante jondo* as potential sublime material. In the programmatic Rima I, as well as in the review, Bécquer rejected the Esproncedan sublime in favor of a minimalist one.[48] Indeed, Rima I and the Ferrán review seem to be holding a dialogue. In the first stanza of Rima I the poet confesses to an innate knowledge of a "gigantic"—read *sublime*, as in Addison's "grand"—and "strange-foreign" hymn, announcing dawn in the night of the soul. In other words, anamnesis occurs, of which the "pages" we read are a faint reflection. This all but ineffable "hymn" can only be transcribed in words that are also "sighs and smiles, colors and [musical] notes" (l. 8). As if responding to this Rima, in his review of *La Soledad*, Bécquer implies that the Andalusian *cante jondo*, Ferrán's model, comes close to being this language. First, Bécquer twice says in the review that "each page [in Ferrán's book] is a sigh, a smile, a tear or a ray of sunlight" (1297, 1301). Second, Bécquer uses the terms "simple" and "concise" with which Lista, following Blair, also characterizes the sublime. What is more, according to Bécquer, the soleá produces "a painful-sorrowful, yet pleasing, impression" (1301) that evokes Edmund Burke's physiological sublime.

Most revealing of all, in establishing the difference on which the review turns, Bécquer distinguishes between his own poetry and declamatory or "civil" verse. But what thus far has not been noticed is that this approximates the distinction between a "greater" and a "lesser" sublime. And the lesser sublime, as Bécquer describes it, returns us to the *cante jondo*. Ideal poetry, as Bécquer remarks,

> is natural [a Lista criterion], brief, [and] crisp, that leaps from the soul like an electric spark, that wounds [our non-sensual capacity for] feeling with a [single] word and dashes off, and naked of artifice, easy within a free form, in touching but one, awakens a thousand ideas that sleep in the bottomless ocean of fantasy (1297).[49]

To appreciate this quote fully one must remember that the "gigantic hymn" of Bécquer's Rima I suggests a sui generis mathematical [although natural] sublime, and that, as he says in his "Introducción sinfónica," there is also a vast and inaccessible mathematical sublime in the poet, such that, while the second is the analogue of the first, the two realms are kept apart by the soul's imprisonment in matter. Thus, although for Bécquer no satisfactory linguistic translation of either sublime is possible, the soleá unleashes a species of harmonics between the abysses within and without. Thus, in a typically romantic paradox, the present separation of inner and outer sublime "proves" they are one and the same.

As critics have noted, to write about the sublime is to write the sublime, and this is what Bécquer does in his *La Soledad* review. But it is also to negotiate the thin line that divides the natural and the textual sublime, which Bécquer also manages to do. Regarding the sublime in his poetry, then, there are abundant references (1) to a "supernatural" and (2) to a "psychological" sublime (the gigantic ocean "beyond" of Rima I; and the bottomless ocean of the *La Soledad* review), as well as (3) to a textual sublime (the dangling hand of the beloved in the soleá). But the sublime also makes an appearance in "A Sketch from Nature" (May 1863) and in the *Cartas literaria a una mujer* (December 1860–April 1861).[50]

Indeed, the sublime is essential to a precise understanding of the first three *Cartas literarias*—wherein the term *love* causes the poet "blockage" and hence becomes an index of the dynamic sublime—and of the relation between the *Cartas* and Rima I. For Bécquer resolved the aporia of ineffableness of Rima I by intimating that he might be able to convey "something" of the sublime hymn to a woman. Indeed, this Rima not only ends with a virtual rewriting of a line from Ferrán's Cantar LXXX ("para cantárselo a solas") with even the same o-a rhyme scheme, it also evokes the mysteriously close relationship—based on their intuitiveness—between women and poets, on which the dialogic relation of the first three of the *Cartas literarias* also depends.

The third and last stanza of Rima I stated: "But it is useless to struggle; there is no cipher / that can encode it [the strange and gigantic hymn], and only, Oh beautiful one! / If I held your hands in mine / would I be able to sing it in your ear if we two were alone." Rather than mere gallantry, this is due, as the first three *Cartas literarias* explain, to the fact that women spontaneously understand the strange, gigantic hymn, but cannot articulate it. Whereas the poet who knows it but fleetingly struggles and ultimately fails to articulate it. Here, in fact, the differences and similarities between the woman and the poet seem a distant echo of Schiller's distinction between the naive and the sentimental, in which the second term is a combination of the qualities of both. However, in modern Spanish poetic tradition there is a thematics according to which woman is a surrogate for "fallen" nature, itself rarely important. Instead, woman represents a kind of "in-its/herself," but at least in Bécquer her eyes are windows that still look out on paradise. Rather than quote from Rima XXXIV, the following passage from "A Sketch from Nature" will illustrate woman's role as substitute for nature and the "naive" in the *Rimas*:

> The true hymn, the poetic word made flesh, was that silent, immobile woman whose glance was never detained by any chance obstacle, whose thoughts could never be contained by any form, whose pupils encompassed the entire horizon, absorbing all its light and reflecting it back again. Until I saw them together, I never completely realized the majesty of these three immensities: the sea, the sky and Julia's bottomless pupils. Scenes ["imágenes"] so gigantic that only those eyes could copy them (773).[51]

Although this ironic "Sketch" seems to denigrate woman's intelligence, Bécquer means to offer a "domesticated" self-deprecating version of the sublime. Like Schiller, he adjusts the naive and the sentimental so that they become naive-sentimental or, in Bécquer's rewriting of the Andalusian *cante jondo*, a highly self-conscious primitivism. The challenge for the poet is to bridge the metaphysical gap between unincarnate ideas and the sensual sphere. For, unlike the perception of the beautiful, the apperception of the sublime is non-sensual, intellectual. Thus, in his poetry Bécquer labors to present "thought" in "images," the better to "mobilize" the passive "imagination"—a simple re-organizer of "fantasy." But only the Genius and the poet ever manage to bridge this gap, as Bécquer says in Rima III. This painful separation into two spheres is in the best Platonic-romantic tradition; the fallenness of the world, the soul's entrapment in matter, the sublime abyss within and without, in addition to anamnesis, are all part of a recycled Neoplatonic philosopheme that Bécquer inherited with the Sevillan poetic tradition of Herrera the Divine. And its elements reappear to different degrees, as a vestigial transhistorical Spanish sublime, in the strong poets (or geniuses) that succeed him down to the present.

This vestigial character explains why the sublime has not been detected even in the *Rimas*. Since for Bécquer a poetic imagination endowed with esemplastic power was inconceivable, in the prose he turned to an expressive rhetoric. Following Lista, he emphasized the figures of passion of apostrophe, exclamation, interrogation, hyperbole, personification, and illusion to convey a special "poetic" state, whether melancholy or exalted. Instead of imagination, Bécquer used these rhetorical figures as signs of his medium-ship, of his capacity as poetic genius to "envision" or "call forth" what he then placed before his readers—as hypotyposis. And, as we have seen, his preferred vehicle for these displays of passionate vision was prose. But in the *Rimas*, where Bécquer had no loco-descriptive poetic tradition to support him, and no available tradition of meditative verse, the psychologistic "internalization" of a "quest romance" was not possible.[52] This is why we have the *Rimas* constructed with Lista's figures of thought: allegory, dialogue, simile, contrast, antithesis, interrogation, ellipsis, repetition, all appropriate to a "reasoning" and a "tranquil," as opposed to an "impassioned" or "agitated," soul.

* * *

If my hypothesis is correct, and recent studies such as Carrillo Alonso's suggest that it is, why has the main effort in explaining the Bécquer phenomenon been expended on foreign—particularly German, French, and English—romantic poetry?[53] As I suggested, Bécquer scholars have been too eager to assimilate him to a non-existent Spanish high romanticism, which has led them to underestimate his eighteenth-century roots, as happened in the case of Larra. That is, to neglect his neoclassical rhetorical training and his knowledge of Addison, Blair, Lista, and Burke, not to mention eighteenth-century treatises on painting. At the same time, for reasons we have seen, critics before Benítez's important study avoided the subject of Bécquer's "traditionalism" and his national-romanticism. But then, because even nineteenth-century aesthetic ideas in Spain are imperfectly known, the sublime itself has been neglected in the study of Bécquer's poetry, essays, legends, and stories. In addition,

Bécquer's "Herderian" enthusiasm for the sublime possibilities of *cante jondo* has created a symbolist or a modern Bécquer. This may have been inevitable with poets, like Juan Ramón Jiménez, who needed a native non-*modernista* precursor, but it made him seem too contemporary. Instead he is another solitary figure, like Espronceda, teetering on a divide that separates both the neoclassical and the preromantic from the romantic.

CHAPTER IV

*L*uis *C*ernuda and the
*R*estitution of *R*omanticism

The possibility that romanticism itself is a "pseudohistorical totalization,"[1] intended to stem the infrangible erosion of material history, has been amply illustrated in chapter 2. But in Spain the precariousness of this literary event is especially striking. There the early nineteenth-century "bourgeois" revolution and its effort at state-making was a partial failure, whereas a conservative nationalistic romanticism enjoyed a relative success. "Spanish romanticism" evolved with such a conservative inflection that even pseudo-high romantic authors like Espronceda and Larra did not escape assimilation.[2] Thus, Spanish historical Romanticism is best approached as the analogue of a contemporary *moderado* liberal social and political compromise.

Given the bald politicization in Spain of the contest between "classic" and "romantic," only a superficial updating of "romantic" poetics proved feasible. To read Lista on the sublime, and observe Espronceda's or Bécquer's practice of it, is to become aware that in Spain's political and social transition from absolute monarchy to parliamentary monarchy (1834–1844)—during the "zenith" of Spanish romanticism—Spanish poetics was only slightly in advance of Addison, Thomson, or Young. As Cernuda—who published a book-length study of English romantic thought—observed, although neoclassic scholars first edited primitive Castilian poetry and romantic ballad collectors first introduced a European taste for "popular" poetry, neither group sparked the regeneration of lyric poetry; instead, a pervasive historical Romanticism that repressed Pindar but embraced Horace, and trafficked anachronistically in the Gothic

99

and the sublime, carried the day.[3] Indeed, no high romantic movement *ever* coalesced in Spain, although, as compensation, the detritus
of European high romanticism appeared piecemeal throughout the
nineteenth and into the twentieth century.

This melodrama of high romanticism withheld, but then disseminated and incorporated, is perfectly illustrated by the poetry of Luis
Cernuda (born, Seville, 1902; died, Mexico City, 1963). In permanent
exile after 1937, Cernuda, on reading the poetry of Hölderlin,
Leopardi and the English romantics, recast his *oeuvre* in a manner
that Abrams would later describe as the romantic "plot." Thus, by
examining Cernuda's poetry we can observe a telling instance of
Spain's sui generis engagement with high romanticism.[4] For if
Bécquer is Spain's classic national-romantic poet, Cernuda is its classic restitutive high romantic one.

Even before Cernuda's death a twofold consensus had emerged
about his work. While young Spanish poets admired him as the most
usefully innovative member of the Guillén-Lorca generation, critics
were elaborating a modern pastoral reading of his work. Ironically,
the productiveness of both these approaches kept critics from noticing the extent to which Cernuda had anticipated Abrams's romantic
plot in his poetry, even though his poetry had constantly been called
"romantic." But thirty years after his death the extent to which
Cernuda's late poetry seems to go well beyond the pastoral-
Abramsian paradigm also requires elucidation.

From Pastoral to Abramsian Paradigm

There is an early and arresting glimpse of Cernuda's entire corpus
in his prose poem "Escrito en el agua," which he discarded after the first
edition of *Ocnos* in 1942. With little extrapolation, it offers an illuminating profile of Cernuda's principle themes before his Mexican sojourn.
Ocnos, the collection's title, even figures forth an image of weaving and
unweaving:

> Since childhood, ever since I can remember, I have always
> searched for what never changed, always longed for the eternal.
> Everything contributed in those early years to preserve in me

the illusion of and belief in permanence: the unchanging family home, the routine of my life. If anything changed, it soon returned to its old ways, so that one thing followed another like the seasons of the year, and behind the apparent diversity I could always discern the ultimate unity.

But childhood ended and I fell into the world. Around me people died and houses fell into ruins. Since at that time I was possessed by the ecstasy of love I didn't even notice this testimony of human mortality. Since I had discovered the secret of eternity, since I had eternity in my spirit, what did I care about anything else? But no sooner did I approach others so as to clasp them to me, in the belief that my desire would give them permanence, than they escaped my embrace and left me empty-handed.

"Later I loved animals, trees (I've loved a poplar, I've loved a white elm), the earth. Everything disappeared, so that a feeling of ephemerality invaded my solitude. I alone seemed to endure the flight of everything. But then, I was suddenly overcome by the idea, fixed and cruel, of my own disappearance, of how I too would absent myself one day.

"Oh God!" I cried out then: "give me eternity." God became the love I had never had in this world, love without rupture, triumphant over the twin-horned cunning of time and death. And I loved God as the incomparable and perfect friend. This was just another dream because there is no God. The dry fallen leaf, crushed under foot as I passed, warned me. A dead bird lying broken-winged and decomposed, told me the same. Consciousness reminded me that one day it would drift into the vastness of nonbeing. And if God didn't exist, how could I exist? I don't exist, even now, a shadow dragging itself along among other shadows, gasping out these hopeless words, an absurd testimony (of whom? for whom?) of my existence.[5]

As we will see, this prose poem is a unique instance of what the poet termed his primordial concern, as well as an almost complete listing of its permutations in his work: the intertwined themes of childhood, love, and nature. The only important themes not alluded to here are those of the artist and society. Now, because we must refer to each of his major themes in order to show the coincidences of Cernuda's version of the pastoral with the Abramsian paradigm, I will begin with the primordial concern itself.[6]

Cernuda's obsessive concern with permanence is the result of a profound sense of existential vertigo, and it causes him to return obsessively to the question of his own mortality. Indeed, no previous Spanish poet has been so forthright in denouncing Christianity. He views it as an empty myth because it demands a docile resignation in the face of death, as in his poem "La adoración de los Magos," in which Christ's birth is related by a skeptical narrator. "La adoración" also reveals Cernuda's characteristic tension between the lack of faith and a nostalgia for belief. His lifelong disposition—like García Lorca he read French translations of Jean Paul Richter—was to view God as a weak Creator exasperated with an unmanageable creation, observing as it plummets toward destruction. Thus, Cernudian man is twice-burdened: he is conscious of finitude and cursed because he can imagine and be jealous of God's prerogative—eternity. One would therefore expect this longing for eternity to be limited to Cernuda's Christian poems. In fact a similar nostalgia characterizes all his mythological poems.

This suggests that Cernuda's subjective experience of eternity is comparable to Blake's and to certain nineteenth-century English nature mystics, in the sense that "eternity is not . . . infinite extension of time . . . [but] a characteristic of the mystical experience . . . [wherein] the experience of time disappears and it is no longer perceived."[7] As the poem "Escrito en el agua" suggests, Cernuda's longing, instead of a will to infinite extension, is a desire to experience aspects of the limited phenomenal world *as eternal*, to linger in its passing moment without an awareness of its passing. That is, it approaches what Nichol Ashton calls a sensitivity to the "epiphanic moment," which becomes the centerpiece of the high romantic and postromantic experience.[8] Described in this way, Cernuda's desire can be easily assimilated to the romantic topos of the child as unaffected by time. Indeed, a typical motif of Cernuda's early poetry is the desire to recapture the childlike experience of the world as pure presence. Thus, because immortality is played down, the same nostalgia can inform Cernuda's mythological and New World pagan poems as well. As Olympian yet "familiar" deities, the ancient gods are not distant for those who believe in them.

Although neither classical nor Christian belief systems reveal an ultimate truth, the poet continues—on behalf of mankind and despite his alienation—to postulate forms of invisible power. Thus, in the course of poems such as "Lázaro," "Quetzalcóatl," and "El elegido," Cernuda develops a complex economy of human and divine exchange. If the evanescence of the contacts with these powers guarantees little, this only seems to increase the poet's delight in the beauties of this world. And because the decay of beauty redounds to the poet's own mortality, a poetry designed to preserve beauty becomes a hedge against general destruction. Here Cernuda discovers for himself a version of Juan Ramón Jiménez's Keatsian "tragic sublime," which had also been borrowed or rediscovered by Pedro Salinas.[9] But since poetry can effect little in this regard, Cernuda was wont to associate the poet with the lamenting Satan in an Arab tale: "Satan—he wrote—is condemned to fall in love with passing things; this is why he weeps, weeps, like the poet, at the loss and destruction of beauty."[10]

There are other links between Cernuda's primordial concern and his poetic vocation: for instance, his almost solipsistic view of the world. In this regard there is another, frequently adduced text, "Words to Accompany a Reading" ("Palabras antes de una lectura"). As Cernuda explains there, he awoke to poetry because he was "wounded" by the beauty of the natural world, as if by that of a human lover. He first became aware of his "poetic instinct" as a spiritual extension of an almost physical desire to become united with that beauty and to "lose himself in that vast body of creation." But since the desire to become part of the Other also had a strong component of possession, and this could not be achieved, a countermovement ensued—*against* the attractive reality. But Cernuda's reaction is even more complex. Because he repeatedly failed to possess, he also concluded that "external reality is an illusion and the only thing certain my desire to possess it" (602).[11] For this reason he gives poetry the task of penetrating illusion, saving appearances, and finally achieving a vision of unity. Although Cernuda seems not to be aware of the connection, this saving of appearances closely approximates Wordsworth's "spots of time," which are the precursors, in the Anglo-American tradition, of Joyce's secular "epiphanies."[12]

Indeed, there are strong intimations in Cernuda of a natural sublime, as well as indications that the poet was a genuine nature mystic, like many nineteenth-century English poets. The many similarities with Wordsworth's poetic and prose declarations confirm this. For instance, their common "union" with nature rarely recurs with the same intensity once the child "falls" into adulthood. In Cernuda's case the result is a characteristic sense of vertigo, together with ontic melancholy and complaints of solitude. His rejection of the temporal condition even deludes him into imagining that "oneness" with "the vast body of creation" might guarantee a degree of ontological stability, just as union with the beloved assuages the pain of separateness. Hence, on the ontic level desire is *eros*, failure, and solitude, whereas on an ontological level, separation, which is permanent, produces melancholy and eventually leads Cernuda to write poetic allegory.

Showing particular originality in the Spanish postromantic context, Cernuda gave a special aura to his poetry of personal experience by recasting it as a "spiritual biography," in the words of Octavio Paz.[13] But like Michelangelo, Manrique, Aldana, Proust, and Gide, Cernuda waxed autobiographical with extreme discretion. His models, he said, had succeeded because they realized the need for a notable depersonalization. Thus, by inserting himself into the Petrarchan *rime* tradition of the book of poems, Cernuda made aspects of his early poetry and of his later prose poetry correspond to the trajectory of his "personal myth" or the "myth of his existence." In other words, the prose poems in *Ocnos* (1942) that deal with childhood and adolescence should be read as a preamble to the poems in *La realidad y el deseo* (*Reality and Desire*), the title he decided on for his collected poems in 1935 and used for the editions of 1936, 1945, and 1958. Like Wordsworth, the Scots poet Edwin Muir, and the American Theodore Roethke, Cernuda freely adapted the myths of Eden, the age of innocence, and the fall, to emplot his own poetic fable of the child who would become a poet.

As we ascertained in "Escrito en el agua," the dominant note of *Ocnos* is of a world undisturbed by clock time, inhabited by the child protagonist, Albanio, in symbiotic union with the natural world. There he enjoys the omnipotence of the child because "reality" almost always conforms to his "desire." But separation overtakes the world after the fall, and the child experiences change and time, and learns that reality always thwarts desire.

In Cernuda's myth of childhood, since only love remains, the fallen child tries to make others permanent through his desire. But without the child's omnipotence the difference between "reality" and "desire" imposes itself. The poetry is thus a stylized autobiography of the struggle to reconcile these two divergent forces. But the solipsistic direction of Cernuda's poetics is not a strategic retreat or evasion. Rather, as with the romantic poets, it is a step in the poetic progression of Albanio's consciousness from *Ocnos* to *Variaciones sobre tema méxicano* (1952).[14] However, the romantic subject-object dialectic also remains blocked in Cernuda and never manages the final de Manian sublimation. In Cernuda's poetics the fall is more decisive than any final synthesis or "marriage." This is a not unexpected climax for his variety of late, sui generis high romanticism.[15]

In this light the prose poems in *Ocnos* can be said to treat aspects of a nuclear Edenic myth. As in Wordsworth's "Intimations of Immortality Ode," its ingredients are timelessness, innocence, early harmony with nature, and a species of anamnesis. However, in contrast with Wordsworth, Cernuda's imperatives of timelessness and immutability require a more circumscribed natural world. It has minimalist, or "Roethkean," temporal and spatial coordinates: the intimate Andalusian "patio," the foot of a staircase, a small garden, a greenhouse. Consequently, this child-poet suffers agoraphobia when he first happens upon the notion of eternity as limitless extension.

Innocence, the second attribute of childhood Eden, derives from the first. There are desires, but they are vague ones, like "le vert paradis des amours enfantines" of Baudelaire's "Moesta et errabunda." Thus persons and things either accede to desire, or with a little imagination can be brought into line. In prose poems such as "Jardín antiguo"—"In that garden, seated by a fountain, you once dreamed of life as inexhaustible fascination"—we have a young Adam balancing on the edge of expulsion; he wants to move on but holds back, wishing to postpone age and the loss of innocence. He senses that the pastoral dream of innocence will prove impossible to sustain in the metropolis.

For after the fall, in the poems of *Un río, un amor* (A River, a Love) (1929) and *Los placeres prohibidos* (Forbidden Pleasures) (1931), the objects of desire are revealed to be young boys and adolescents. If in

Ocnos the child's desires are innocent, the young boy and the adolescent as love object now appear, without irony, as a way of recovering innocence. As Cernuda writes, "Seeing them dash off that way provokes a double desire, because in addition to your admiration for the youth of others there is also nostalgia for your own, now gone, painfully drawing you after those creatures that still possess it."[16].

However, this superposition of the lover and of one's own lost youth, in part based on the desire to recover innocence, creates an obvious dilemma. In Cernuda's surrealist love poetry there is the explicit wish that innocence not be destroyed; and yet its "corruption" seems desired, inevitable. Hence the poems, "De qué país eres tú?" ("From What Country Are You?")," "Tu pequeña figura" ("Your Small Form,") and especially "Qué ruido tan triste" ("What a Sad Sound") where the contrast between corrupted adult love and the innocent love of young boys is thematized:

> Qué ruido tan triste el que hacen dos cuerpos cuando se aman,
> Parece como el viento que se mece en otoño
> Sobre adolescentes mutilados,
> Mientras las manos llueven,
> Manos ligeras, manos egoístas, manos obscenas,
> Cataratas de manos que fueron un día
> Flores en el jardín de un diminuto bolsillo.[17]

> What a sad sound two bodies make when they love,
> It sounds like the wind stirring in autumn
> Over mutilated adolescents,
> While hands rain down,
> Deft hands, egotistical hands, obscene hands,
> Cataracts of hands that one day were
> Flowers in the garden of tiny trouser pockets.

Finally, in perfect complementarity with *Ocnos*, Cernuda wrote *Variaciones* (1952), to commemorate his late rediscovery of an "Andalusian" nature in the landscape of México. There, after his long exile in northern countries—England, North America—he managed again to apprehend the moment as eternal present through a new experience of love. The desire to reunite with the image of his younger self, a theme on which so many of the poems of the earlier *Vivir sin estar viviendo* (*Living but Not Alive*) had turned, could be satisfied, and the difference between "realidad" and "deseo" made to disappear. In "El Patio," from *Ocnos*, he describes this apparent recovery of the paradise from before the fall:

> The man you now rediscover in this embrace with the child he was, and the only existence each has is rooted in a small, secret, silent Andalusian corner of the world. You realize then that in living this other half of life you simply recapture at last, in the present, your own lost childhood, when the child, in a state of grace, was already master of what the man later, in the wake of countless mistakes, doubts and missteps, has had to struggle to regain.[18]

In a critical essay Cernuda once praised Salvador Rueda, author of *Himno a la Carne* (1890), for breaking with the Spanish Petrachan tradition and writing poetry about sexual love.[19] Certainly, in his forthrightness Cernuda far outdistanced other homosexual members of the poetic Generation of 1927. In this regard neither Aleixandre nor García Lorca were Cernuda's contemporaries, but Shakespeare and Michaelangelo. As Cernuda wrote in "El acorde" ("The Chord"): "[You] can neither perceive, desire nor understand anything unless it is first sexual, then heartfelt, and finally mental."[20] Written over a period of thirty years Cernuda's love poetry is a meditation on desire's ultimate significance. Since we only need to confirm its connection with his central concern, its treatment here can be brief.

When Cernuda's love declares its homoerotic nature, there are ramifications in his other subthemes; this occurs first in the three books of love poems, *Un río, una amor*, *Los placeres prohibidos*, and *Donde habite el olvido* (*Where Forgetfulness Lives*). But even in these surrealist poems there are intimations of a metaphysical conception of love, as in the verse "Because desire is a question whose answer no one knows" (RD, 178), or in "It is not love that dies,/ But we ourselves" (RD, 210).

Now, to reconcile the altered subtheme of love with that of childhood, we need only remember that nearly all Cernuda's love poetry converges in the Narcissus myth as recycled by Freud and Gide. For example, there is the desire of Narcissus to become one with his reflection, which corresponds to Cernuda's worship of the adolescent (Narcissus is the *puer aeternus* par excellence)—so that, like the theme of childhood, this subtheme also marks a partial recovery of childhood. For love after the fall also offers intimations of immortality. At least, it seems to free Cernuda from space, time, and an aging self. However, the union of Narcissus with his image is too fleeting. Therefore, in the course of reading *La realidad y el deseo* the amount of experiential or anecdotal material diminishes and a fragmented, increasingly abstract conception of love takes its place. It is likely that Cernuda's lifelong "*pudor*" ("reserve") kept him from rivaling the sexual candor of his hero the Neoplatonist poet Francisco Aldana.

In the early *Un río, un amor* and *Los placeres prohibidos* the homosexual love that is also presented as a potential act of social revolution is for the first time the central theme. An ethical and political force is attributed to homosexual love as Cernuda establishes a typically pastoral contrast between Sansueña (Málaga), conducive to love—a place of sun, beaches, and sea—and its antithesis, the metropolis, hostile to love of any kind. This remains the "Shelleyan," ethical message of Cernuda's love poetry. In the third collection of love poems, *Donde habite el olvido*—the title borrowed from Bécquer—there is a distillation of an affair with a lover named Serafín.[21] These poems repeatedly suggest that since desire is infinite it cannot be satisfied. In the poem "El invisible muro" ("The Invisible Wall")—the beloved body—Cernuda claims that the ideal union is soul with soul, as in the case of the Spaniard Aldana with the English Metaphysicals. But in the kingdom of this world the separation of individuals is total. And since sexual love itself is one cause of this impasse, *Donde habite el olvido* closes with a half-serious renunciation in favor of nature. Its last poem, "Los fantasmas del deseo" ("The Phantoms of Desire") contains the lines,

> Nimbos de juventud, cabellos rubios o sombríos,
> Rizosos, lánguidos como una primavera,
> Sobre cuerpos cobrizos, sobre radiantes cuerpos

que tanto he amado inútilmente,
No es en vosotros donde la vida está, sino en la tierra,
En la tierra que aguarda, aguarda siempre
Con sus labios tendidos, con sus brazos abiertos.[22]

Aureoles of youth, chestnut or blond hair,
curly or long and smooth as spring,
fallen over bronzed bodies, radiant bodies
that I have loved so much to no purpose,
life is not to be found in you, but in this earth,
in the earth that waits, waits always
with lips offered, and with open arms.

Consequently, Cernuda's next collection of poems, written in 1934–1935, received the title *Invocaciones*, and the previous renunciation of "bronzed bodies" is somewhat qualified. As Cernuda wrote in the Introduction to his Hölderlin translations, published in *Cruz y Raya*, "There will always be those surprised by the lovely diversity of nature and the horrible ordinariness of man. Nevertheless, nature always seems to require the presence of a lovely and different being [or person] among its perennial unwitting beauties. Hence the secret permanence of pagan myths. . . ."[23] The "gods" praised in Cernuda's subsequent Hölderlin-inspired odes—an Andalusian boy, a young sailor—are celebrated as incarnations of nature's need for local deities. Thus, an apostrophe to one of the "Olympic heroes" reads:

Expresión armoniosa de aquel mismo paraje,
entre los ateridos fantasmas que habitan nuestro mundo.
Eras tú una verdad,
Sola verdad que busco,
Más que verdad de amor, verdad de vida. . . .[24]

Harmonious expression of that same landscape,
Among all the frightened phantoms inhabiting our world,
You were one true thing,
The only truth I look for,
More than the truth of love, the truth of life. . . .

Throughout his extended exile in England, United States, and Mexico, which began in 1938, meditative love poems continued to appear in the successive editions of *La realidad y el deseo*. Longer poems like "Vereda del Cuco" ("The Cuckoo's Path"), "La ventana" ("The Window"), and, in México, a second "Bécquerian" cycle of outstanding love poems, "Poema para un cuerpo" ("Poems For A Body") constitute, together with "El éxtasis" ("The Ecstasy"), the summation of Cernuda's love poetry. In the significantly titled poem "The Ecstasy," he describes a heaven that would allow an idyll modeled on Garcilaso's Platonic-pastoral world and on Herrera's Eclogues. Here the lover is acknowledged to be also a reflection of the poet's own youth, not simply a god—a final confirmation that successive lovers are finally seen as reflections of "Narcissus" himself. "The Ecstasy" closes a series of poems about unsatisfied desire because it depicts a sublime fusion of his young self with the lover, in or beyond death. If, throughout the entire *La realidad y el deseo*, desire is frustrated and the longing for union a constant, through each act of love Cernuda-Narcissus joins momentarily with his reflection, completing himself and indirectly uniting himself with nature. True to the Metaphysical tradition, these poems concentrate on the mind-body paradoxes inherent in human love.

Finally, since Eden is the alpha and omega of the Cernudian world, our thematic review calls for some reference to Eden as symbolic space. We have already mentioned the attributes of timelessness and innocence. A third attribute, and vital center of the theme of nature, is a momentary oneness with the world. In reviewing the theme of love, we saw how nature played a compensatory role, like the image of the child. Similarly, in the postlapsarian metropolitan world, nature is also perceived as an inspirited "Other," with which the poet longs to be reunited, since it connotes timeless, unconscious existence.

Unlike Cernuda's other main themes, a nonpastoral nature only appears during his post-1937 English exile. In his earlier surrealist period the dominant note was a guardedly extroverted poetry of homosexual love and social revolution. During his wartime exile in England, in reduced spiritual, emotional, and economic circumstances, his childhood in Seville began to reappear in new prose poems, a genre he had first employed in the surrealist period. Together with its scenery, childhood is sanctified as a haven from the Civil War and then from the World War in Europe. It is even likely that this new thematics also served to mask Cernuda's disillusionment with the Communist takeover of the Republican cause, which he experienced firsthand in Valencia, where several friends were apparently liquidated.

In any event, the wish to reexperience the protective natural world associated with childhood led to an idealization of minimal existence, or *vita minima,* as Ortega termed this (French romantic) "Andalusian" ideal. As the autobiographical protagonist of *Ocnos,* Albanio provided a vehicle during exile in wartime Britain for exploring and refining his un-Spanish sensitivity to the English countryside. Guided by Albanio the reader discovers the first fragments of Cernuda's self-legend. Thus *Ocnos* offers a Wordsworthian double perspective in which Albanio-Cernuda experiences and exemplifies the existential ideal, and Cernuda-Albanio comments on it. Following its appearance first in *Ocnos,* a romantic thematics of nature also appeared in new poems destined for *La realidad y el deseo.*

Not only does Cernuda's English nature poetry surprise for its unaccustomed concreteness; in the new poems nature also becomes a Platonic magister, a poetic strategy undoubtedly gleaned from his reading of Wordsworth. The daffodils of the former's "I Wandered Lonely as a Cloud" are "mortal" when confronted as spectacle, but this is only a superficial revelation. By contrast, when evoked "in tranquillity," their dance is perceived as the epiphany of a divinely organized universe. Cernuda exhibits a similarly complex view of nature: it exhibits oxymoronic qualities, it is mutable and unchanging, sympathetic and yet alien. While in both Wordsworth and Cernuda there are sublime or epiphanic experiences, in the latter a tragic, non-egotistical, sublime is evident. Here is a passage from Cernuda's "Violets" to illustrate his attempt to see what he terms "la unidad del ser disperso" ("the [underlying] unity of dispersed being"), or else "las bodas espirituales de lo mortal y lo sobrenatural" ("the spiritual wedding of the mortal and the supernatural"):

> Leves, mojadas, melodiosas,
> Su oscura luz morada insinuándose
> Tal perla vegetal tras verdes valvas,
> Son un grito de marzo, un sortilegio
> De alas nacientes por el aire tibio.[25]

Weightless, damp, melodious,
Their dark purple light asserting itself
Like vegetable pearls set among green half-shells,
They are March calling out, the bewitchment
Of new-born wings in the warm air.

Instead of any overt declaration, Cernuda's ideolect indicates that these flowers are harbingers of the sublimity he senses at hand. "Mortal" in their real individuality, the violets grow in memory, once they are gathered to his inner eye. But first they are real violets, then epiphanic ones. As indices of nature as physis Cernuda's poems now contain references to the four elements—especially to air, water, fire—as well as to fountains, centenary trees, and supernatural presences like the enigmatic "new-born wings" in "Violetas."

In the prose poem "The Poet and His Myths" from *Ocnos*, Cernuda explained that his interest in Greek mythology reflects his nostalgia for "a corporeal and spiritual harmony broken and exiled centuries ago. . . ." But, as we have seen, adult nostalgia also seems to have its poetic compensations. In addition to an infrequently requited love, there is a memory of the childhood Eden, in which body and soul, sensual desire and *vita minima*, are not yet at odds. These possibilities make separation from the One of nature and ontological instability somewhat bearable.

This is also why the two symmetrical collections of prose poems, *Ocnos* and *Variaciones sobre tema mexicano*, enclose Cernuda's poetic autobiography, the first evocative of a prelapsarian world, the second commemorating a new conjunction of the Edenic elements that were scattered by the fall. The landscape and climate of México were perceived as a satisfactory approximation of Andalusia, and with a new lover to receive the projection of his own youth, Cernuda reactivated memories of his earliest Spanish years at the same time he imagined a new conjunction with nature. The protagonist of *Variaciones*—still called Albanio—is at last delivered from existential solitude and ontological vertigo. Now the mystical "chord" reappears, and through sexual possession of the beloved—also a mirror of nature—the poet recovers "aquel vasto cuerpo de la creación" ("that great body of creation"). This is detailed in the prose poem "La posesión," where a mystical chord is "struck" corporeally and spiritually. The new physical embrace encompasses "the [Mexican] earth," "a dark firm body," and the very pulse of life (*Variaciones*, 649–650).

Taken together these three major articulations of Cernuda's unifying theme constitute his "spiritual biography." They describe three intersecting elliptical circles that depart from and return to the primordial concern. In addition to these major themes, in *Luis Cernuda: el poeta en su leyenda* (1965;1972) (Madrid: Castalia, 1995) I discussed two secondary ones: the question of literary posterity, and Sansueña, or Cernuda's reflections on Spanish history from exile. In both cases these subthemes generate poems that seem logical extensions of the central themes. Yet, despite their surface coherence the pastoral-romantic and Abramsian readings still fail to provide Cernuda's poetry with a satisfactory closure.

A seemingly exhaustive pastoral-autobiographical mapping of the poetry cannot account for Cernuda's late and abundant display of what García Berrio has called the "imaginario cultural" ("cultural imagination").[26] Literary figures, musicians, cultural artifacts, the very title of Cernuda's last collection of poems—*La Desolación de la Quimera*—suggest a later poetic concern with his place in the literary canon. Evidently, when his high romantic "plot" ceased to generate new poems, Cernuda could not help sharing his doubts about the reception of his life's work.

Although his poetic generation began under the aegis of Góngora, the Andalusian members were also drawn to Garcilaso's and André Gide's very different versions of the pastoral. Thus Cernuda, Prados, and Altolaguirre—and later Vicente Aleixandre (in *Sombra del paraíso* [1944])—developed a romantic-symbolist version of the pastoral. This generational context, together with Cernuda's book-length study of the English romantic poets, accounts for his original reinterpretation of the Platonic-romantic thematics of childhood, love, and nature, and for his spontaneous incorporation of a romantic "plot" like the one later described by M. H. Abrams in *Natural Supernaturalism*.

And indeed, except for a seminal essay by Octavio Paz and studies by Derek Harris, all early readings of Cernuda's poetry emphasized the conciliatory aspects of this pastoral mode. It took the "Novísimos," a heterogeneous grouping of young Spanish poets, to discover and highlight Cernuda's "culturalism."[27] This was their label for an impersonal poetry containing few, or no, autobiographical allusions, as in the extraordinary "Augustan" poetry of Guillermo Carnero. Thus a new metaleptic focus on Cernuda's "cultural imagination" drew attention to the problem of closure in the pastoral-Abramsian understanding of his work. However, as we shall now see, it is still possible to account for Cernuda's "culturalist" poems, without forfeiting either his indubitable Abramsian modeling or his importance as the best examplar of restitutive high romanticism.

Cernuda's Postromantic Sublime

Les allégories sont au domaine de la pensée ce que les ruines son au domain des choses.
—Walter Benjamin[28]

When Cernuda chose the title *La realidad y el deseo* for his collected poems in 1935–1936, there is no indication that he thought of himself as a pastoral poet. He fancied himself a sexual revolutionary, a sometime surrealist, and a PCE (Partido Comunista de España) fellow traveler. But in exile, as he composed the prose poems of *Ocnos*, he recast his life in the plot of Eden, the fall, and, on a higher level, reconciliation. Seemingly at the nadir of existence, Cernuda was moved by nostalgia and exile to assume a Schellingesque, or Wordsworthian, romanticism, and to configure his poetic existence according to a substantially pastoral design. This approach to romanticism accorded with his early ideal of "lyrical haughtiness," absorbed during his youthful reading of Chateaubriand—*Le Dernier Abencérage, Atala, René*—and his adult daydreams of Gidean terrestrial paradises.

But as the titles for the collections of poetry that Cernuda wrote after 1942 show—*Como quien espera el alba* (*Like Someone Waiting for the Dawn*) for the poetry written between 1941–1944, *Vivir sin estar viviendo* (*Living but Not Alive*) for that of 1944–1949, and *Con las horas contadas* (*With But a Few Hours Left*) for the poetry of 1950–1956—the poet's spiritual animus changed while in exile, as did his existential ideal. Instead of seeking reconciliation and tranquillity, his poetry became more philosophic and discursive, but also more celebratory and sublime. Cernuda's struggle with passing time began to take on a more impersonal character; he still reacted to the destruction of beauty, but now the destruction was accepted as tragic and sublime. His poetic persona seems to have become reconciled to an authentic temporal destiny, which eventuates in a drier, non-mimetic, even allegorical conception of the poem. The problem is that this last modulation seems to contradict the pastoral-romantic reading of his poetry. Nevertheless, a different critical synthesis is still possible that will account for this new departure in Cernuda's long trajectory of more than three hundred poems, as well as prose poems, short stories, autobiographical writings, critical essays, and glosses on his own poetry. The most economical approach will be through the reexamination of Cernuda's central prose statements of poetic intent.

Here the text most frequently cited has been the fundamental "Words to Accompany a Reading" in its 1941 version.[29] This time, in discussing it, I will be careful to distinguish between the lived, pre-poetic experiences to which this type of preamble refers, and his explicit poetics. In this case, Cernuda begins by observing that he was first aware that he would write poetry when he felt a sudden heightened perception of "the beauty and attractiveness of the surrounding world." This made him feel an imperious, almost painful need to escape the confines of the self into the Other of creation, which was repeatedly frustrated. Consequently, as we saw, he realized that he harbored two contradictory impulses: towards, and away from, reality. As Cernuda says: The momentary possession of reality seemed to ratify his existence but, since it was rare, he reacted against the attraction. Even though he calls this "conflict between reality and desire" "the essence of the poetic problem," it must really be an *existential* problem that he would like to resolve through his poetry, thereby "allowing the discovery of an image of the totality of the world [that is] hidden." Indeed, he refers to the "preliminary experience" or "conflict . . . [that] the poet tries to solve *in his work*" (602) (my emphasis). Clearly, Cernuda has imported a pre-poetic preoccupation *into* the poetry.

Both his initial self-dramatization and his awareness of a "hiatus between inspiration and [creative] work" place him on the threshold of the sublime, as do his repeated professions of expressive inadequacy.[30] In fact, a significant correlation will emerge as he begins to promote "values" such as the inescapability of self, the impossibility of possessing reality, and the ineffability and unpresentability of nature as a totality.

A rift between life and poetry similarly appears a decade later in "La Poesía" from *Ocnos* in which Cernuda refers to the experience he calls the "acorde" ("the chord"); that is, the sudden epiphanic apperception of "a reality different from everyday reality," with the concomitant conviction that "it was not enough for the other reality to be different, but *something winged and divine must also accompany and surround it.*"[31] However, whether in the lived pre-poetic experience or in poetry, the invariant is the *impossibility* of expressing or representing the "world's hidden loveliness." This is why Cernuda says he feels condemned to "silently enjoy and suffer this bitter and divine drunkenness, *uncommunicable and ineffable.*"[32] In other words, especially in the poetry, expressive failure is a virtual certainty. Thus, he says, the poet must live with "failure and defeat" and with "the dramatic drunkenness of defeat."[33]

This invocation of a hovering protective grace is a faint echo of his early poetic deployment of the ancient gods. We have already recalled his remark that favorite landscapes such as Sansueña-Málaga cry out for such deities. Like Hölderlin, he felt himself to be "a living echo of pagan forces buried nowadays"; and he also believed that his "pale nostalgia over the disappearance of those gods" marked him as different in the modern world.[34] But in addition, the divinities in Cernuda's poetry also carry additional allegorical freight: if they are first indices of the ineffable beauty and mystery of the world, they are also personifications with which Cernuda attempts to "fix the transitory loveliness of the world he perceives, [by] attaching it to the invisible world he intuits. . . ."[35] Despite the metaphorical nature of these substitutions, Cernuda's divinities must be considered allegorical since their very necessity as poetic "materializations" denounces his failure to conjoin the visible and the invisible.[36]

That is why, according to Cernuda, as a poet he feels kinship with the Prince of Darkness. As he says, "when [the poet] collapses, defeated in unequal strife, his enamored voice, like Satan's . . . bewails the loss of what it loves" (605). Thus, despite his statements to the contrary, Cernuda's poetics is troubled by an unbridgeable ontological rift between the visible and the invisible. Therefore, when he affirms that *in poetry* "the supernatural and human unite in a spiritual marriage, from which come celestial beings" (604), he voices what is at best a sought-after ideal.[37]

The point of underscoring these contradictions in Cernuda's poetics is to show that to the extent that "Palabras antes de una lectura" is a poetics, and not a description of pre-poetic experiences, it signals a "poetics of failure." Here I believe that what the poet calls his daemon has confounded the poet and his critics. That is, critics have accepted without demurring his importation of "the [mystical] chord" *into* the poetics, whereas it properly belongs in a future biography—along with his nature mysticism. Therefore, what ultimately needs explaining is Cernuda's poetics of failure, which contravenes and points beyond the supposed conciliations of the pastoral.

As Cernuda insists in his pronouncements, only in and through such conflict is any glimpse of the image hidden behind appearances possible. Of what precisely is this an image? Of the oneness of all there is, a pledge that the entities we daily perceive are at least remnants of an exploded whole. Moreover, in the best romantic tradition the poet mediates in this conflict on behalf of mankind. But instead of striving to close the divide, as in the pastoral mode, insistence on the conflict itself is the means of expressing it. However, by subtracting the nature mystic from the poet's persona, we also undercut the basis for Cernuda's classification as a romantic-symbolist. That is, whatever support "the chord" appeared to lend a Schellingesque reading of Cernuda's poetry has now been read-dressed to his biography. And since the metaphysics of romanticism-symbolism at least implies the possibility of uniting subject and object in an absolute I, Cernuda no longer fits the model of Schellingesque romanticism. Before, when the relevant statements were read as part of a pastoral-Abramsian poetics, Cernuda seemed a romantic symbolist like Baudelaire, but now as a demystified poet of *non*-conciliation his poetry requires a different ensign.

The Satan figure and the notion of a "daemonic power," on which Cernuda seems to have staked his poetic truth, are highly suggestive in this regard. Is there a place for Satan on Cernuda's Mount Olympus with the other ancient gods? Satan would make an unusual addition, albeit quite in keeping with Cernuda's reputation as a "poète maudit." Besides, except for the "natural supernatural" figures—the Andalusian youth, the young sailor—the gods that do appear in Cernuda's poems are also "fallen" ones, "silent witnesses of a vanished past."[38] Here is an illustration:

La piedra cariada, el mármol corroído,
Es descomposición del dios, segura
De consumarse bajo el aire, como
Bajo la tierra la del hombre;
Ambos, el dios y el hombre, iguales
Ante el ultraje igual del azar y del tiempo
Cuyo poder los rige, y aceptada
La humildad de perderse en el olvido.[39]

The stone pitted, the eroded marble,
The decomposition of a god, its wearing
Away made certain by the wind, just as
Man's is assured beneath the earth,
Both made equal, god and man,
Through a similar savaging by chance and time
Whose powers subject them, accepting
The humiliation of becoming lost in oblivion.

Thus, the ancient gods really instantiate no "spiritual marriage" between the human and the supernatural, any more than Satan does. This helps us reassess the role of Satan in the poetics and the poetry. While in a biography of Cernuda the mystical chord would have considerable authority, in the poetics and the poetry it is much less important than Cernuda's evocations of the antithetical figure of Satan. For he says:

I feel a daemonic power hovering over me, over us all. In one of Blake's engravings, a very beautiful Satan, with the splendid force of Michelangelo's figures, spreads his membranous wings over the dark world, while he droops his head toward one shoulder with an expression of immense pain and sadness, [and] treads Job's body underfoot. . . . This part of the engraving is as vague as the diabolic figure is clear. As though this figure alone mattered and the rest were contrast; it seems a veiled symbol. A friend showed me a reproduction of this engraving. By extraordinary coincidence, that same day I read this answer by a Muslim theologian. . . .[40]

Before completing this quotation, there are three intriguing ancillary points to remember: first, Cernuda's engraving by Blake was almost certainly inspired by Milton's Satan; second, Edmund Burke also uses the example of Milton's Satan in exemplifying the sublime in *Philosophical Inquiry into the Origin of our Ideas of the Sublime and Beautiful*; and, of course, what Cernuda calls "a veiled symbol" is more properly an allegorical figure. Now consider the rest of the quotation. Cernuda describes a "daemonic power" and "a vast and indefinite power that controls our destinies." Recall that this power is interwoven with his "poetic beliefs" and that both the daemonic and the poetic resist further definition (604). The poet next explains why, in response to a question about the sound of a flute, the Muslim theologian said, "It is Satan's lamentation for the world." Here is the rest of the quotation in its 1935 version:

> Satan, the commentarist adds, was condemned to fall in love with things that perish and so he weeps; he weeps for the destruction and loss of beauty. Like the poet, like man.
>
> . . . .
>
> But this lament does not exclude a kind of terrible joy, nor does it exclude Good and Evil; rather each extreme needs the other in order to create a harmony surpassing our weak and petty desires.
>
> . . . .
>
> Good and Evil, lamentation and joy; yes, all is required, all necessary; it all vibrates in that Satanic voice weeping for the world, everything is the expression of that dark force that tries to grasp and hold the perishable.[41]

This figure of Satan is more than the allegory of perishability; it is an allegory of allegory itself, which helps explain the conundrum of the "cultural imagination" in Cernuda's later poetry. Although Cernuda's culturalism is "never excessive or ostentatious," certain critics have seen it as a sign of diminished poetic power.[42] Instead, it announces a predisposition to the allegorical, as in the later poetry of Antonio Machado and the later Yeats. Moreover, Cernuda's strategem recalls medieval allegory in which, according to Benjamin, "the pagan gods mingled with

Christian demonology."[43] If we expand the notion of Cernuda's "cultural-ism" in this way, as a strategic displacement in the direction of allegory, it is again compatible with his romantic self-emplotment. For the latter also reveals the allegorist's "awareness of the ephemerality of things and the desire to make them eternal. . ." (241). However, if we resist this notion of allegory, it can only be because, as Benjamin suggests, we see it as threatening the comforting mystifications of romantic symbolism.[44] This is the ultimate meaning of Cernuda's "culturalism": it is a late alle-gorical reflection of his own experience with romantic symbolism. This new understanding makes it possible to align both his early romantic self-emplotment and his "culturalism" with an overarching romantic pre-occupation with "saying" the ineffable, which brings us to Cernuda's ver-sion of the postromantic sublime.

In treating Cernuda's poetics, we began by separating his experien-tial apprenticeship from his poetic theory and practice. The result was the discovery of a poetics of failure, conveyed in terms of sharp, even violent, contrasts between reality and desire, between good and evil, between sorrow and joy. And, as we noted, Cernuda himself speaks of a "terrible joy" in the face of failure and of the "dramatic drunkenness of failure," as he struggles to exorcise the "dark daemonic force that con-trols the world" (605). Now, however, his peculiar poetics of failure can perhaps be recast in the image of the sublime.

Here, as with Bécquer, contrast and difference indicate the threshold of the ineffable. For example, to complete an earlier quotation from "La Poesía" in *Ocnos*, the other "entity" must be not only different, but "something winged and divine must attend and surround it, *like the tremulous nimbus around a luminous point*."[45] Here the contrast is represent-ed by the slightest degree of difference in illumination. The reason why "something winged and divine" *must* attend it is that this "bitter, divine drunkenness [is] uncommunicable and ineffable." This reminds us of the effect of "blockage" associated by Longinus and others with the sublime. Hence, we can appreciate the poet's appropriate allegorical use of Blake's or Milton's Satan, a borrowing uniquely situated to suggest, in its literary sublimity, the veneration, the fear, and the rapture the poet feels for beauty, together with his sense of impotence before its ephemerality. But this veneration, fear, and rapture, so essential to the experience of epiphany in Cernuda, are ultimately positive in their result. For as Kant says, "In our aesthetic judgment, nature is not considered sublime because it is awesome but because it awakens our power (which is not that of nature) in ourselves." The sentiment of the sublime is then felt when we substitute an inner adjustment between two faculties for an external one between subject and object. As Lyotard explains:

> In the tradition of subject-philosophy . . . a conflict develops between the faculties of a subject, that of conceiving a thing and that of "presenting" it. . . . The sublime is a different feeling. It comes about when . . . the imagination fails and cannot present an object.
>
> . . . .
>
> We can conceive of the absolutely great, the absolutely powerful, but any presentation of an object destined to "make visible" this magnitude . . . seems woefully insufficient to us. These are Ideas that cannot be presented. . . . We could say that they are "unpresentable."[46]

Equally important, Cernuda's sublime involves a Burkean combination of pleasure and pain.[47] Yet Cernuda's sublime is not Kantian, but postromantic or modern. For he only believes there can be a "negative presentation" of what he conceives but cannot make visible—hence his late thematics of past art, artists, music, and ruins, as allegories of the ineffable.[48]

How else could one present the unpresentable in poetry? Lyotard appeals, in addressing this question, to Kant's notion of "negative presentation." But, as Lacoue-Labarthe objects, this makes the unpresentable into something substantive. Besides, a presentation can only "indicate its beyond in what it presents, or by the selfsame act of presenting."[49] Thus, when presentation seeks to indicate its beyond, either a difference between the presentation and the presented occurs, or we sense that a limit has been reached. In which case, attention passes to the "something" that retreats and hides "in the act of presentation."[50]

In this way, in a postromantic, modern sublime, the problem of "representation" alludes to a difference between presentation and the presented that is a token of the rift between Being and entities. Now we can see that in the poetics of failure there was a premonition of Cernuda's sublime; in its contrasts, in its antithetical extremes, there was also the allusion to "something" that withdraws. Thus his poetics of failure should be seen as directed toward Being as "the *transcendens* pure and simple" (Heidegger, *Sein und Zeit*, Sec. 7, 62),[51] not toward the smooth and untroubled romantic correspondence between consciousness and a pantheistic nature, and not to the metaphysical division that reenters literature with high or Schellingesque romanticism, which reaches all the way to French symbolism and Hispanic *modernismo*. Cernuda's concern is with the distinct question of Being as nature and nature as sacred (Hölderlin), and as Hegel's unsayable "mere Being" (*nur Sein*). That is, Cernuda's poetics aims at something similar to what Hölderlin spoke of as the "marvelous all-present," in brief, "something" that sustains all, and about which the poet would like to speak, but that cannot be *said* in any poem. Here in a single, brief declaration is a reasonably complete account of Cernuda's postromantic or modern sublime:

> Besides, how express with words what is inexpressible? Words are alive, and hence betray; what they express as true and pure today, is tomorrow false and dead. They must be used, taking into account their limitation, so that in translating it, they do not falsify too much the intuited truth we try to express with them. At least, perhaps they can convey part of it, be impregnated with meaning that only the poet suggests: the mystery of creation, the hidden beauty of the world.[52]

This passage condenses a lifelong poetic struggle to represent the ineffable, a struggle already implied in the title of Cernuda's first collection of poems, *Perfil del aire* (*Profile of the Wind*) (1927).

CHAPTER V

On "Resolute Repetition": A Methodological Conclusion

About myself and how I have been thus far, how far I have stayed worthy of you and my friends, also what I am engaged in and what I will produce, as little as it is, about all that I will write to you next time from the neighborhood of your Spain. . . .[1]
—Hölderlin, Letter to Böhlendorff, 4 December 1801

In his revisionary essay "Romanticism and Anti–Self-Consciousness," Geoffrey Hartman characterizes the subject of romantic poetry as looking back "at a transcended stage and [coming] to grips with the fact of self-alienation." But Spain's version of historical Romanticism did not allow for alienation, retrospection, or imaginary projections into the future. Thus, because the crucial psycho-cultural event of romantic alienation never occurred, there could be no return to innocence by way of experience, no redemption via nature or imagination in Spain. This makes it easier to understand Spain's compensatory fixation on its national history and its failure to relate the past to any present or future national project. Indeed, apart from such literary exceptions as Bécquer's sublime prose and poetry, few points in Spain's "unreturned" historical Romanticism invited later poets to "resolute repetition" or "futural" dialogue.

❧ Of course, there is no sign that Hölderlin ever crossed the Pyrenees into Spain, and in any case no further letters reached Böhlendorff until November 1802, after his friend's difficult return north from Bordeaux. But if Hölderlin *had* entered Spain and given his X-ray mind, the sharply different letter he might have written would have recorded a radical view of "romantic" Spain. Indeed, that letter might have read more like the following:

My Dear Friend!

I have not written you for a long time, have been meanwhile in Spain and have seen the sad, solitary earth, the shep-
herds of Castile and individual beauties, men and women, who
have grown up in the anxiety of patriotic doubt and hunger.

The tremendous element, the fire of the sky and the silence
of the people, their life within nature, and their limitedness and
satisfaction has continually affected me, and as it is said of the
heroes, so I may say that Apollo has struck me.

In the area nearest Africa, I have been interested in the
wild, the martial [character], the purely male for which the light
of life becomes immediate in eyes and limbs and which, in the
intimation of death, feels like a [moment of] virtuosity, and
which fulfills its thirst for knowledge.

The athletic [character] of the Spanish people in the ruins
of the ancient spirit made me more familiar with the specific
essence of the Greeks; I became acquainted with their nature
and their wisdom, their body, the way in which they grew within their climate, and the rule by which they protected their exu-
berant genius against the violence of the elements.

This determined their popularity, their habit to assume a
foreign character and communicate themselves through them;
hence they possess their individually proper [character] which
appears alive to the extent that supreme understanding is, in the
Greek sense, reflexive power; and this becomes intelligible for us
if we comprehend the heroic body of the Greeks; [reflexive
power] is tenderness, like our popularity.

Beholding the ancients [Spaniards] has given me an impression which renders intelligible to me not only the Greeks but
generally the highest in art.

My dear friend! I think that we will not comment [on] the
poets up to our time, but that the form of poetry [Sangart] in
general will take a different character, and that therefore we do
not succeed because, since the Greeks, we have again begun to
poetize in patriotic natural, and in properly original manner.

If you would just write to me soon. I need your pure tone. The psyche among friends, the origination of thoughts in conversation and correspondence is necessary for artists. Otherwise we have nobody for ourselves, but he belongs to the sacred image we produce. Farewell.

Your
H.

If instead of the lovely Dordogne Valley Hölderlin had actually traveled much farther south into arid Castile, his most famous letter might have contained the alterations I have introduced, for he would have seen that the Spaniards were not ordinary Hesperians, not Western as were other Europeans. Moreover, if we contrast this letter, even as originally written, with his poem "The Ister," the median term in the poem *between* Greece and Hesperia—that is, Africa, Egypt, or the Orient—is absent from it as it is from our account in chapter 2, section 3 "European Romanticism in Ruins."[2] This suggests that if Hölderlin *had* gone to Spain he would have witnessed more than the Greeks' nature as well as how they suffered (from Homer's desire for self-consciousness). For, as de Man says, "[Hölderlin] was able to imagine Greek virtues and happiness since [he] knew about them through the nostalgia [he] had for them, but [he could not] know the extent of *their* desire for the clarity that *we* possess."[3]

In Spain, which for eight hundred years had been *part* of the Orient, he might have seen firsthand both the Greeks' *nature*, which was the Orient's foreign, and the Greeks' foreign, which was the Orient's nature. That is, Hölderlin could have discovered in Spain an approximation of what Hesperia ought to have been—a replica of the Orient—if Greece had not interposed itself between Hesperia and the Orient. In Spain Hölderlin might also have seen a Hesperia that "had grown up in the anxiety of patriotic doubt," in other words, had become cathected *between* the Orient and "Greece"—that is, not on Greece but a on version of its *own* past. He would have seen a distorted Hesperia, then, torn between two different natures and two different foreigns, a Hesperia that, instead of being separated from itself (the Orient) by Greece, managed to reject itself qua Orient and hence reject Hesperianism (Hesperia = the Orient).[4]

In terms of history and culture this would mean that, with its intimate experience of the Orient, Spain might have become the model Hesperian culture. But because it initially shared in the classical heritage as well, it became stretched, Tantalus-like, between the two. Hence Spain was by turns too prone to usurp the gods' portion, too "mystical" (the "sacred fire" and "holy passion" [or the Orient's foreign]), but also too "popular," too terre-à-terre (nostalgia for the natural object [or Greece's native]).[5]

It is not surprising, then, in terms of literary history, that the dominant Spanish romanticism was a historical Romanticism, which paid homage to Spain's medieval and early Renaissance periods and much less attention to the classical world. This is partly because, beginning in the sixteenth century and for two hundred years after, Spain itself seemed to rival the glory that was Rome. The Spanish monarchy had become, according to Anthony Pagden, "the largest single political entity in Europe."[6] But while Spain in the sixteenth century was the "self-assured champion (and the exporter) of Christian cultural values, the secular arm of the Papacy, and the sole guardian of political stability within Europe," by the late eighteenth century Europeans perceived a weak and ailing Spain as "the apotheosis of wilful, institutionally enforced Ignorance." (Pagden).

Finally, for much of the nineteenth century, Spain was occupied by its own and foreign troops. But German and French romantics had already begun turning Spain's abysmal ranking with the Enlightenment to its advantage. Spain's apparent ignorance and rejection of the Enlightenment, its elephantine circling around a dead past, were precisely what F. and A. W. Schlegel found to lionize. And so Spain delighted anew in Calderón and Cervantes, who were now ranked on a par with Dante and Shakespeare. Moreover, in addition to the foreign romantics, Spain's historical Romantics prepared the terrain for its romantic historians, who from a nineteenth-century bourgeois perspective, refurbished the historithemes of the Reconquest, the Catholic monarchy, and a Spain unified ab initio: all collective myths the bourgeoisie required to insulate the conservative values of a moderate Liberal parliamentary monarchy. Nor were these would-be national values merely sociopolitical ones; they equally effected the selection of the literary canon and the formulation of a new national literary history.

Spain, indeed, set a record for intentionally living under the weight of a misconstrued and inert past—that of its world dominance and gradual decline. This way of life meant that Spain had to bear the responsibility for its own decline, but it also meant that Spain never suffered the trauma of severance from its classical past the way Italy and Greece did. Although its national myths were inventions or magnifications like those of other countries, the distortions worked by Spanish historiography failed in modern times to win or maintain statewide acceptance. This poses the following questions about *literary* history: What is the genuine "native" of Spain's past? And what would an authentic interpretive relationship to it be?

The answers to both these queries depend on the notion of "resolute repetition," noticed in chapter 2. This can best be developed by referring to Heidegger on ordinary (or *inauthentic)* "world-historical" history. As he describes it in *Being and Time*,

> The transcendence of the world has a temporal [not a spatial] foundation; and by reason of this, the *world-historical* is, in every case, already 'Objectively' there in the historizing of existing Being-in-the-world, [but] *without being grasped historiologically* [i.e., it remains unwritten]. And because factical Dasein, in falling, is absorbed in that with which it concerns itself, it understands its history *world-historically* in the first instance. And because, further, the ordinary understanding of Being understands 'Being' as presence-at-hand ["things objectively there] without further differentiation, the Being of the *world-historical* is experienced and interpreted in the sense of something present-at-hand which comes along, has presence, and then disappears.[7]

Now, what Heidegger calls "factical Dasein" (Dasein immersed in its material situation) is the "subjective" pole of this same world-historicality, which inevitably suffers a quotidian dispersal in the "they." But when, on the one hand, through a "resoluteness," which "constitutes the *loyalty* of existence to its own Self," Dasein comes to realize that both world-historicality and lostness in the "they" are actually a flight from death (and instead turns back), then, according to Heidegger, a different practice of resoluteness can make a temporality of *authentic* historicality possible. The latter, "as the moment of vision of anticipatory repetition, *deprives* the 'today' of its character *as present*, and weans one from the conventionalities of the 'they'."[8] If, on the other hand, as with the practitioners of historical Romanticism, "one's existence is inauthentically historical, it is loaded down with the legacy of a 'past' which has become unrecognizable. . . ."

This means that quotidian or inauthentic history implies a present-bound, too-reverential view of the past as monumental time, or time gone by; whereas the really *authentic temporality*—which is finite—*is itself authentic historicality*. Thus, rather than being *in* history, authentic Dasein is literally the *making* of history—and, as we have seen, the *poetic* making of history. But only an entity that is "futural," and "free for its death," which is to say, "equiprimordially in the process of *having-been*, can by handing down to itself the possibility it has inherited, take over its own thrownness and be *in the moment of vision* for 'its time'."[9] Of course, this would be as true for a given community ("Spain") as for an individual Dasein; in fact "*destiny*" is how Heidegger designates the historizing of a community, of a people.[10]

Nevertheless, as Heidegger reminds us, such a national destiny is by no means "fateful," and it need not be passively accepted; instead, "in the depths of its Being Dasein *is* itself fate,"[11] due to the coexistence of *choice* with inheritance. In sorting through the choices thrown up by the past, through active "resolute repetition" Dasein carries out what Heidegger's translators, Macquarrie and Robinson, call a "conversation with the past," one in which the past "proposes certain possibilities for adoption, but in which one [Dasein, the community] makes a rejoinder to this proposal by 'reciprocating' with the proposal of other possibilities as a sort of rebuke to the past, which one now disavows."[12] Since, as we have seen, nineteenth-century historiography failed to join in an adversative relationship with past history—for example, on the "romantic" question of the "national" diversity of Spain—this kind of genuine dialogue only appeared in Spanish historiography during the Republican lull before the Spanish Civil War. The dialogue was among soon-to-be exiled literary critics and historians such as Américo Castro and Claudio Sánchez Albornoz—who began the vindication of Spain's Others (Jews,

Arabs, Basques)—or among the "regional" historians and ethnographers, the great J. Vicens Vives and, of course, Pere Bosch Gimpera. But with rare exceptions, like Patxot y Ferrer and Almirall, nineteenth-century Spanish writers usually followed in the footsteps of the inauthentic "they" of the historical Romantic writers of poetry, drama, and the novel. In fact, until they were replaced by Pérez Galdós's *Episodios nacionales*, the General Histories of Spain were one of the principal instruments of *moderado* bourgeois indoctrination.

Another especially serious consequence of historical Romanticism's servile view of its fictionalized past was that no authentic *"futural"* "poetic tradition" appeared to link nineteenth and twentieth century poetry to the past. This is what enabled national-romantic writers like Zorrilla and Campoamor to carry the message of historical Romanticism almost to the doors of the twentieth century. Fortunately, however, this did not preclude the possibility of elective affinities established across time between poet and poet,[13] similar, perhaps, to the "resolute repetition(s)" that underpin Paul de Man's "historical poetics" and that cause him to typify European romanticism as the affinities later writers asserted with Rousseau. Indeed, no *world-historical* "period," "movement," or even "national literature" *could* predict all the encounters that might pertain according to Heidegger's model of "going back to the possibilities of the Dasein that has-been-there." At the same time, this Heideggerian proposition provides a sound philosophical basis for a "futural" diachronic literary history on the order of Harold Bloom's too psychologistic model of romantic *transumptio* as Oedipal mayhem.[14] As Christopher Fynsk explains, Bloom's

> "scene of primal instruction" may occur in an encounter between two Daseins somehow present to one another, or it may occur through the address of one Dasein to another by way of some form of record or monument. Heidegger argues, in this latter respect, that any existential project is also a history that takes the form of an active interpretation—a kind of counterinterpretation—of *a possibility of existence that has been*, an existence that presents itself as a kind of model to Dasein.[15]

As a provisional illustration we have seen how early German romantics encountered classical Greece as difference—then, in the extreme
case of Hölderlin, how it reappeared as unknowable and hence inim-
itable. Finally, Paul de Man emphasized a severing from the unmediated
experience of romanticism's "passing away" as constitutive "of our own
consciousness of temporality."[16] This recalls his related proposition that
meditation on the *demise* of classical antiquity produced romantic neo-
Hellenism; as well as his late view that lyric poetry is mourning and its
basic figure prosopopeia. Although in either case the intentionality of
resolute repetition is condemned to "fall short," there are still poetic
remainders that are "futural."[17] This is also why de Man's essay, "The
Temptation of Permanence," concluded by asserting that

> Far from being antihistorical, the poetic act (in the general
> sense that includes all the arts) is the quintessential historical
> act: [the one] through which we become conscious of the divid-
> ed character of our being, and consequently, of the necessity of
> fulfilling it, of accomplishing it in time, instead of undergoing it
> in eternity.[18]

Finally, given the inauthenticity, and the ultimate "they-ness" of
nineteenth-century Spanish history, as well as the seeming impossibility
of closing off the period designated "romanticism," we also have a final
obligation to ask if the literary historical labels, Neoclassical, Romantic,
Modernista, and Vanguard, have not hidden from view a non-stratified,
non-Castile-centric, antitradition of modern poetry: a different
"Spanish" poetic tradition that consists of poets interpreting previous
national *and foreign* poets and which not only renounced its world-historical "foreign"—romantic nationalism's eternally unified Spain, with
its dogmatic "realism"—but also accomplished a "native turning back"
(*CW,* 74) to a pluri-nationalism and a consequential international literary diversity. In other words, this antitradition may be a de facto poetic
tradition that would consist of Bécquer involved in "resolute repetition"
of Espronceda; Juan Ramón Jiménez, Pedro Salinas, Jorge Guillén, and
Luis Cernuda in "resolute" exchange with Bécquer but also with Heine,
Shelley, Leopardi, Keats, Hölderlin and Wordsworth, Emerson, Poe,
Baudelaire, Valéry, Whitman, and Joan Maragall.

But a final word of caution. Hölderlin's model is not to be taken as a historical scheme. Its use here has been heuristic. We forget at our peril that beneath such designations as Hölderlin's model of the return, historical Romanticism, or Romanticism itself, there is only, "the ceaseless erosion of monstrous material history," "wearing away and wearing down," (ruining) everything.[19]

*N*otes
*B*ibliography
*I*ndex

NOTES

(Unless otherwise indicated, all translations from Spanish in the text and in the notes are my own.)

Introduction

1. ("Románticos somos. . . . ¿Quién que Es, no es romántico?") Rubén Darío, "La canción de los pinos," [El Canto Errante], *Poesía*, Preface by Angel Rama (Caracas: Biblioteca Ayacucho, 1977), 334–335.

2. For this use of *restitution* I am indebted to Enrico Mario Santí's essay "Sor Juana, Octavio Paz and the Poetics of Restitution," *IJHL* 1, no. 2 (1993): 101–129, in which he details the technical differences between restoration and restitution. He addresses the ideology of restitution apparent in current colonial studies. I discuss the restitution of high romanticism in Spain (of more than, and other than, what was originally there), as opposed to its restoration.

3. See E. Allison Peers, *A History of the Romantic Movement in Spain* (Cambridge: Cambridge University Press, 1940), 1:80–81.

4. She published *Follas novas* in 1880. This raises the political question of whether we are to consider her a "Spanish" or a Galician poet, or both.

5. See my "Towards a Revisionary Theory of Spanish Romanticism," *Revista de Estudios Hispánicos* 28 (1994): 294–297.

6. Not dealt with here are Catalán, Basque, Galician, and Aragonese romanticism. It is not by chance that the axis of modern "Spanish" poetry, as in the "Generation of 1927," replicates the political-administrative axis of the Castilian-Andalusian oligarchy that has ruled modern Spain. The other "tributary" axis lies between Catalunya and the Basque country. If we examine the more famous "students" at the Residencia de Estudiantes in the 20s, we have, besides the Andalusians, also Salvador

Dalí, of the Catalán haute bourgeoisie, and Buñuel from Calanda. (Nearby Zaragoza is an important midpoint on the industrial-intellectual Catalán-Basque axis.) This axis is represented in post–Franco Spain by writers such as Juan Benet Goitia and Juan Goytisolo (from the Euskera: *Goi, Goi[tu]: high, to overcome*).

7. In her *Romantics, Rebels and Reactionaries* (Oxford: Oxford University Press, 1981), 7, 185, Marilyn Butler contrasts "idealizing" "philosophical" critics (and comparatists) with "literary historians" and "non-philosophical literary scholars." Her examples of the former are René Wellek, Harold Bloom, and M. H. Abrams.

8. Philippe Lacoue-Labarthe and Jean-Luc Nancy, *L'absolu littéraire: Théorie de la littérature allemand* (Paris: Editions du Seuil, 1979), 42. See also Maurice Blanchot's essay, "L'Atheneum," in *L'entretien infini* (Paris: Éditions Gallimard, 1969), 515–527.

Chapter 1

1. "Historical Romanticism" succeeded as a political ideology because it was perfect at "hiding the real contradictions and . . . *reconstituting* on an imaginary level a relatively coherent discourse" on behalf of moderate miberalism. See Nicos Poulantzas, *Political Power and Social Classes*, trans. Timothy O'Hagan (London: New Left Books, 1973), 207. "Moderate liberal" translates the Spanish political term *moderado*; see note 6, infra.

2. See Donald L. Shaw, "The Anti-Romantic Reaction in Spain," *Modern Language Review* 63 (1968): 606–611.

3. P. Aullón de Haro, *La poesía del siglo XIX* (Madrid: Editorial Playor, 1982), 21.

4. A. de Haro, *La poesía del siglo XIX*, 22.

5. Derek Flitter, *Spanish Romantic Literary Theory and Criticism* (Cambridge: Cambridge University Press, 1992), "Conclusions: The mid-century," 185.

6. Eventually the liberals divided into a *Moderado* and a *Progresista* Party, although the differences were of little moment. I use *moderado* or *moderado* mentality to refer to the conservative-liberal community of thought that pervaded nineteenth-century liberal politics through the Restoration (1874–1923).

7. Navas-Ruiz, *El romanticismo español*, 3d edition (Madrid, 1982); Vicente Llorens, *Liberales y románticos: Una emigración española en Inglaterra (1823–34)* (Mexico City: El Colegio de México, 1954); *Romanticismo y realismo*, ed. Iris M. Zavala, vol 5 of *Historia y crítica de la literatura española*, ed. Francisco Rico (Barcelona: Crítica, 1982), part 1: "Románticos y liberales, Introducción."

8. See Richard Cardwell, "*Don Alvaro* or the Force of Cosmic Injustice," *Studies in Romanticism* 12 (1973): 559–579.

9. This notion originated with Donald L. Shaw, "Towards an Understanding of Spanish Romanticism," *Modern Language Review* 58 (1963): 190–195, and was developed by Richard A. Cardwell, "The Persistence of Romantic Thought in Spain," *Modern Language Review* 65 (1970): 803–812.

10. I designate as *high* romanticism one centered on, in Abrams' words, "the secularization of inherited theological ideas and ways of thinking" (*Natural Supernaturalism*, 12). I develop this point in chapter 2.

11. Susan Kirkpatrick, *Las Románticas: Women Writers and Subjectivity in Spain, 1835–50* (Berkeley: University of California Press, 1989), 48.

12. Kirkpatrick, *Las románticas*, 41–42.

13. Virgil Nemoianu, *The Taming of Romanticism: European Literature and the Age of Biedermeier* (Cambridge, Mass.: Harvard University Press, 1984), 27.

14. See chapter 19 of his *José de Espronceda y su tiempo*, tr. Laura Roca (Barcelona: Editorial Crítica, 1989). Mesonero Romanos's satire, "El romanticismo y los románticos" appeared in the *Semanario* in 1837 and is probably an imitation of Musset's *Lettres de Dupuis et Cotonet*. On "national-romanticism" see note 29, infra.

15. Nemoianu, *The Taming of Romanticism*, 28–29, 38–39.

16. See Hans Juretschke, *Origen doctrinal y génesis del romanticismo español* (Madrid: Ateneo, 1954); Derek Flitter, *Spanish Romantic Literary Theory . . .* ; and Robert Marrast, ed. *José de Espronceda.*

17. Blanco Valdés says of this *moderado* hegemony: "Only interrupted briefly with the parentheses of 1854–1856 and 1868–1874, it continued through the long period of the Restoration until the general crisis of the system of bourgeois oligarchy that took place in the Second Republic. As Jordi Solé and Eliseo Aja maintain, 'the construction of the

system of processes and institutions we call the contemporary Spanish state fundamentally took place under two Constitutions: those of 1845 and of 1876, that is, of the *moderado* period and the Restoration'" (Roberto L. Blanco Valdés, *Rey, Cortes y fuerza armada en los orígenes de la España liberal, 1808–1823* [Madrid: Siglo XXI, 1988], 474, n.1).

18. For what follows, see Antonio Elorza's "La ideología moderada en el trienio liberal," *La modernización política en España (Ensayos de historia del pensamiento político* (Madrid: Ediciones Endymion, 1990), 141–236.

19. Elorza, *La modernización política,* 142.

20. See Antonio-Miguel Bernal, "Antiguo Régimen y transformación social," in *Antiguo Régimen y liberalismo: Homenaje a Miguel Artola,* vol. 1, *Visiones Generales,* ed. A. M. Bernal, B. Clavero, E. Fernández de Pinedo, et. al. (Madrid: Alianza Editorial/Ediciones de la Universidad Autónoma de Madrid, 1994), 69–86; especially, 69–70.

21. Bernal, "Antiguo Régimen," 70. See also 76–81.

22. Another important actor was the military, which as Marx observed joined the fray because it was the only sector of the ancien régime affected—in a revolutionary sense—by the War of Independence. On Spanish "praetorianism," as opposed to militarism, see Valdés, *Rey, Cortes y fuerza armada,* 474–517.

23. Elorza, *La modernización política,* 142.

24. Cited in ibid., 143. For details of the bourgeoisie-nobility pact see Carlos Marichal, *La revolución liberal y los primeros partidos políticos en España, 1834–1844* (Madrid: Ediciones Cátedra, 1980), especially 146–150.

25. Vicens Vives, "El romanticismo en la historia," in *El romanticismo,* ed. David T. Gies (Madrid: Taurus Ediciones, 1989), 162–163.

26. Vicens Vives, "El romanticismo," 163.

27. See Pedro Tedde de Lorca, "Revolución liberal y crecimiento económico en la España del siglo XIX," in *Antiguo Régimen y liberalismo: Homenaje a Miguel Artola,* vol. 1, *Visiones Generales,* ed. A. M. Bernal et al. (Madrid: Alianza Editorial/Ediciones de la Universidad Autónoma de Madrid, 1994). For a summary of liberal policy, including the effects of disentailment on the nation at large, see 31–49; especially 48–49.

28. Alberto Gil Novales, "Las contradicciones de la revolución bur-

guesa" in the collective volume, *La revolución burguesa en España* (Madrid: Editorial Universidad Complutense, 1985), 45–58.

29. The component of *"romantic nationalism"* (Jover Zamora) that I include as basic to national-romanticism amounts to a "free-floating" nationalism adrift between the past and the present, which ultimately conflates the two. For example, in speaking of the mid-century historian, Modesto Lafuente, who perfectly exemplifies this national-romanticism, Tomás y Valiente notes his "españolismo fundamentalista y ahistórico," and Jover Zamora his "nationalism-centralism."

30. See José María Jover Zamora, *La civilización española a mediados del Siglo XIX* (Madrid: Espasa-Calpe, 1992), 144.

31. Derek Flitter, *Spanish Romantic Literary Theory*, 3.

32. The result was a *formal* historicism, which made historical Romanticism an excellent foil. Marrast suggests that, although this historicism may have been aestheticist, its failure to distinguish past clearly from present made it especially appropriate as an instrument of *moderado* ideology.

33. ("In politics, for example, the ancient was called *despotism*, and the new *liberty*; and the names were as ill-defined and unclear as *Classicism* and *Romanticism* used for the ancient and the new in literature . . . [But] if the things themselves were unclear, how could their names, the formulas for the things, be any clearer?") Cited in Salvador García, *Las Ideas Literarias en España entre 1840 y 1850* (Berkeley: University of California Press, 1971), 5.

34. Nemoianu, *The Taming of Romanticism*, 23–25, not "Preromanticism" as forerunner of a Spanish high romanticism, but as a not-yet romanticism (see Brown, *Preromanticism*, 2).

35. Elorza, *La modernización política*, 141–143.

36. See Hans Juretschke, *Vida, obra y pensamiento de Alberto Lista* (Madrid: C.S.I.C., 1951) for a well-documented intellectual biography. Elorza concludes of the *Gaceta de Bayona* that its "character as an official organ of Fernando VII was disguised by a bland criticism of administrative measures and [the lack of] freedom of expression in literary matters" (*La modernización política*, 217–218).

37. Cited in Elorza, *La modernización política*, 148.

38. Cited in Marrast, *José de Espronceda*, 32.

39. Elorza, *La modernización política*, 187.

40. Juretschke, *Vida, obra*, 254–55, 513.

41. Ibid., 329–330.

42. Marrast, *José de Espronceda*, 72.

43. From the article, "Reflexiones sobre la dramática española de los siglos XVI y XVII," *El Censor* 7, no. 38, 24 April 1821, 131, cited by Marrast, *José de Espronceda*, 75.

44. I am indebted to Derek Flitter for his discussion of the influence of Durán on Lista (*Spanish Romantic Literary Theory*, 40–42); Marrast suggests that Lista in turn influenced Durán with his own *Discurso* of 1828, given on entering the Real Academia de la Historia (*José de Espronceda*, 229–230).

45. Flitter, *Spanish Romantic Literary Theory*, 78–79.

46. Flitter observes that: "Given the fact that Schlegelian ideas were strongly associated with Roman Catholicism and monarchy, and given also Lista's own involvement in both constitutional and absolutist administrations, the change in tone between 1821 and 1828 could be attributed to political expediency" (41).

47. Marrast, *José de Espronceda*, 233.

48. Ibid., 234.

49. Ibid., 266–267.

50. About *El Siglo* editorial policy, Marrast comments: "The editors of *El Siglo* limit themselves to repeated affirmations of grand principles, especially regarding individual liberties and rights; they called for their urgent enforcing in Spain, but without ever stopping to consider practical matters about their application, *which they never envisioned as extending to all citizens*" (282, the italics in my translation are my own).

51. Marrast, *José de Espronceda*, 268. See pp. 268–286 for an account of the sparring between *La Estrella* and *El Siglo* and the difficulties of editing an "anti-government" paper.

52. Marrast, *José de Espronceda*, 314.

53. See Ibid., 190.

54. Elsewhere by "(poetic) epistemology" I mean the epistemological *self*-understanding of a poetic text, as opposed to its author's extra-poetic statments about it. A conspicuous "romantic" example of the latter would be Bécquer's *Cartas literarias a una mujer* (1860–1861).

55. Marrast, *José de Espronceda*, 108, 241–242.

56. Romero Tobar, *Panorama crítico del romanticismo español* (Madrid: Castalia, 1994), 129, draws attention to this frontispiece.

57. See Romero Tobar, *Panorama crítico*, 367. From her most famous "Autobiography" [1839] it is clear that Gertrudis Gómez de Avellaneda (1814–1873) and her young friends avidly read Gothic novels.

58. Anne Williams, *Art of Darkness: A Poetics of Gothic* (Chicago: University of Chicago Press, 1995), 105. My intention here is not to ridicule Don Félix de Montemar but to urge that his constituent parts are not two but three: besides the legendary womanizer of the national Don Juan myth, and the gnoseological rebel-quester, associated in Spain with Byron's name, there is *also* a Male Gothic substrate. Indeed, the compulsive braggadocio of Espronceda's hero seems closer to the Gothic villain than to anything else. The critics' consensus is that Espronceda failed to form a coherent figure from the first two (see Juan Luis Alborg, *Historia de la Literatura Española*. Vol. 4, *El Romanticismo* (Madrid: Gredos, 1980), 329.

59. Williams, *Art of Darkness*, 105–106.

60. By ideolect I mean Antonio García Berrio's "endo-retórica." Two articles on lexical-epistemological matters in Espronceda are David T. Gies, "Visión, ilusión y sueño romántico en la poesía de Espronceda" in *Cuadernos de filología*, 3, Facultad de Filología, Universidad de Valencia, 1983, 63–84, and Leonardo Romero Tobar, "Sobre fantasía e imaginación en los primeros románticos españoles," *Homenaje a Pedro Sainz Rodríguez* (Madrid: FUE, 2, 1986), 581–593.

61. Janet Todd, *Sensibility: An Introduction* (London: Methuen, 1986), 55.

62. References are to Espronceda, *El Estudiante de Salamanca / El diablo mundo*, ed. Robert Marrast (Madrid: Castalia, 1982).

63. Martin Price, "The Theatre of Mind: Edward Young and James Thomson," in *Poets of Sensibility and the Sublime*, ed. with an introduction by Harold Bloom (New York: Chelsea House, 1986), 71–87.

64. See Marrast, *José de Espronceda*, 495–503.

65. Derek Flitter, *Spanish Romantic Literary Theory*, 130–131, 62, 177.

66. For the notion of "romantic historians," see M. Moreno Alonso, *Historiografía romántica española; introducción al estudio de la historia en el siglo XIX* (Seville: Universidad de Sevilla, 1979).

67. Paloma Cirujano Marín, Teresa Elgorriaga Planés, Juan Sisinio

Pérez Garzón, *Historiografía y nacionalismo: 1834–1868* (Madrid: Centro de Estudios Históricos, C.S.I.C., 1985), 71.

68. This "national" bourgeoisie, as it emerged, fused with the aristocracy of the ancien régime, while what we now call the "middle classes" (here, more precisely, the petty bourgeoisie) lived with the constant economic threat of proletarianization, according to Vicens Vives. The "people" or "nation" was regularly excluded. Except during the War of Independence and the Civil War of 1936–1939, the term "Spanish nation" never included, or referred to, "the masses." On the subsequent decrease in the inclusive use of "nación" and "nación española" in successive constitutions, see Francisco Tomás y Valiente, "Lo que no sabemos acerca del Estado liberal," *Antiguo Régimen y liberalismo: Homenaje a Miguel Artola*, vol. 1, *Visiones Generales*, ed. A. M. Bernal et al. (Madrid: Alianza Editorial/Ediciones de la Universidad Autónoma de Madrid, 1994), 138–142.

69. Flitter, *Spanish Romantic Literary Theory*, 48.

70. What Marrast says of historical Romanticism is even more true of the "national-romantic" semi-attachment to the Middle Ages exhibited in the General Histories of Spain. Their "turn toward the past was essentially reactionary, to the extent that it produced in those who experienced it a pasivity, or else a lyrical exaltation" (*José de Espronceda*, 418–419).

71. Jover Zamora, *La civilización española*, 145.

72. Ibid., 149–152.

73. Vicente Llorens calls *Venganza catalana* "an appeal to patriotic feelings, an apotheosis of the Spanish nation;" it traded on the O'Donnell government's various military adventures beginning in 1859. According to Llorens these were: "A series of military actions that we view today as manifestations of the colonial expansionism of the Spanish bourgeoisie of that period, similar to that of the French bourgeoisie under Napoleon III" (*El romanticismo español* [Madrid: Editorial Castalia, 1989], 399–400).

74. Jover Zamora, *La civilización española*, 153.

75. Remember that here and throughout "liberal" refers to Spanish "heterodox liberalism" (Manuel Ballbé), launched at the Cadiz Cortes of 1812. On fundamental questions of centralism and nationalism, liberalism was actively opposed not only by royalists and traditionalists in arms,

but also by "exaltados," democrats, federalists, and even by Carlists and republicans, armed and conspiring together against the liberals.

76. Paloma Cirujano Marín et al., *Historiografía y nacionalismo*, 86.

77. Ibid., 85.

78. Ibid., 73.

79. See my essay, "La invención de la Reconquista," *Bitarte* 7 (December 1995): 39–48.

80. Paloma Cirujano Marín et al., *Historiografía y nacionalismo*, 86.

81. Ibid., *Historiografía y nacionalismo*, 88.

82. In Spanish historiography "Neo-Visigothic" refers to the invention at the end of the ninth century of royal Visigothic ancestors for the Astur-Leonese monarchs, as a tactic for legitimizing them vis-à-vis their new Western subjects. This fictitious Visigothic link was later applied to the Castilian rulers between 1234 and 1246 by the Navarrese prelate Rodrigo Ximénez de Rada, who served Fernando III. As Diego Catalán writes, Ximénez de Rada "appropriated the [spurious] ideal of the Neogothic unity of Spain from the Leonese chronicals and, by a careful Castilianization of the stories, was the first to align Castile's desire to be "ruler of a kingdom" with the aforementioned national enterprise." See his "Ensayo introductorio" to Ramón Menéndez Pidal, *Los españoles en la historia*, 2d edition (Madrid: Espasa Calpe, 1987), 28–29.

83. Quoted in Paloma Cirujano Marín et al., *Historiografía y nacionalismo*, 88.

84. Ibid., 89–90.

85. Jover Zamora, *La civilización española*, 165.

86. See Francisco Tomás y Valiente's "Lo que no sabemos acerca del Estado Liberal," in *Antiguo Régimen y liberalismo*, 137–145; and Vicente Fernández Benítez, *Carlismo y rebeldía campesina: Un estudio sobre la conflictividad social en Cantabria durante la crisis final del Antiguo Régimen* (Madrid: Siglo XXI de España Editores/Ayuntamiento de Torrelavega, 1988).

87. See Menéndez Pidal's *Los españoles en la historia,* ed. Diego Catalán (Madrid: Espasa Calpe, 1987), 176. This essay-introduction was required reading during the Franco years, whereas Pere Bosch Gimpera's inaugural address was published for the first time in 1978. For the complete "Text de la lliçó inaugural del curs 1937–38 de la Universitat de València," see P. Bosch Gimpera, *Espanya*, pròleg de Miquel Tarradell (Barcelona: Ediciones 62, 1978).

88. ("Because Castile was strength, decency and measure, Spain exists still as an historical category"), from *Castilla la gentil* (México, 1944), 26. For an analysis of Americo Castro's historiographic existentialism and his Generation of 1898 Castile-centrism, see Eugenio Asensio, *La España imaginada de Américo Castro* (Barcelona: El Albir, 1976).

89. Edmund L. King, "What is Spanish Romanticism?" *Studies in Romanticism*, 2 (Autumn 1962): 11. See also E. Inman Fox, "En torno a la actitud romántica de la Generación de 1898," *Humanitas, Anuario de Estudios Humanísticos de la Universidad de Nuevo León*, 5 (1964): 235–243.

90. See Vicente Cacho Viú, "Ortega y el espíritu del '98," *Revista de Occidente* (1985); and Antonio Ramos-Gascón's destabilization of the concept in "Historiología e invención historiográfica: El caso del 98" in *Eutopías: Teorías/Historia/Discurso* 3, no. 1 (1987): 79–101.

91. See, at the same time, the profound criticism of Basque nationalism from within by Jon Juaristi, *El linaje de Aitor: La invención de la tradición fasca* (Madrid: Taurus, 1987); Mikel Azurmendi, *Nombrar, embrujar: Para una historia del sometimiento de la cultura oral en el País Vasco* (Irún: Alberdania, 1993); Carlos Martínez Gorriarán, *Casa, provincia, rey: Para una historia de la cultura del poder en el País Vasco* (Irún: Alberdania, 1993); and Carlos M. Gorriarán and Imanol Agirre Arriaga, *Estética de la diferencia: El arte vasco y el problema de la identidad, 1882–1966* (Irún: Alberdania/Galería Altxerri, 1995).

92. This unveiling of the "Castilian" nationalist component of the Generation of 1898 helps clarify the relation between Manuel Machado's *modernista* poem "Castilla" and Antonio Machado's *Campos de Castilla*. On late Castilian nationalism see E. Inman Fox's illuminating "Spain as Castile: The Invention of a National Culture," *Working Paper no. 4 of the Spanish Studies Round Table*, University of Illinois at Chicago, delivered 1/29/1993. I am indebted to Professor Fox for the suggestive phrase "Spain as Castile" and for the terms "Castile-centric" and "Castilophile." See *La invención de España: Naciónalismo liberal e identidad nacional* (Madrid: Cátedra, 1997).

93. "Authoritarian contradictions" refers to the fact that the Spanish bourgeoisie, the weak partner in a pact with the landed nobility, made matters even worse with its "praetorianism." As Antonio Elorza observes in *La modernización política en España*, 141–145, (and I para-

phrase) the bourgeoisie became trapped in a vicious circle formed by these facts: (a) it was not evenly distributed throughout the country; (b) in order to become the dominant class, it needed a popular, artisan, and proletarian base to counter the regressive torque of the ancien régime; and (c) the repeated interruption of *democratic* liberal plans by authoritarian *moderado* liberalism, which came to power in 1837, 1843, 1856, and in 1874, because its political model better matched the converging economic interests at the end of the ancien régime.

94. I am indebted to E. Inman Fox, leading Generation of 1898 and Azorín scholar, for bringing these uncollected essays to my attention in 1988. See Fox's new edition of *Castilla* (Madrid: Espasa Calpe, 1991) for other examples. Azorín's literary and political essays perfectly illustrate the encoding of the past in terms of the present that characterizes romantic nationalism.

95. On modern nationalism and national literature see Vassilis Lambropoulis, *Literature as National Institution: Studies in the Politics of Modern Greek Criticism* (Princeton: Princeton University Press, 1988), and Gregory Jusdanis, *Belated Modernity and Aesthetic Culture: Inventing National Literature* (Minneapolis: University of Minnesota Press, 1991).

96. This deference to the Spanish peasant in literature and politics is a "compensatory" liberal myth, partially examined by Dian Fox in two books on kingship in Golden Age theater. There it is a distant harbinger of the demagogic politics of the Franco era. On Franco's "ideología de la soberanía del campesinado," see M. Pérez Ledesma, *Estabilidad y conflicto social: España, de los iberos al 14-D* (Madrid: Editorial Nerea, 1990), 225.

97. According to Richard Fletcher, *The Quest for El Cid* (New York: Knopf, 1990), in 1863 Don Ramón's uncle, the Marqués de Pidal, bought the only extant MS of the Poem of the Cid. Fletcher also notes that the publication of the essay "Los españoles en la historia," coincided with Menéndez Pidal's rehabilitation under Franco and restoration to the presidency of the Academy (204–205).

98. Ramón Menéndez Pidal, *Los españoles en la historia* (Madrid: Espasa-Calpe, 1987), 71.

99. Ramón Menéndez Pidal, "Los españoles en la historia," *Historia General de la literaturas hispánicas*, vol. 1 (Madrid: Espasa Calpe, 1947), xxvii.

100. See *National Separatism*, ed. William H. Colin (University of Wales Press, 1982).

101. See Francesc-X. Blay, *Espanya horizontal (introducció al concepte històric d'Espanya* (Valencia: Nau llibres, 1982), 19–20.

102. As in post–1978 Constitution parlance, "historical nationalisms" refers to the Basque, Catalan, and Galician autonomies, because of their foral and other "ancient" "rights," and because they received Autonomy Statues under the Second Republic.

103. See my *Nacionalismos y Transición: Euskadi, Catalunya, España* (San Sebastián: Editorial Txertoa, 1988), chapter 1 and Epilogue, for a less cursory treatment of Ortega's diagnosis of failed Castilian hegemony.

104. Quoted in Antonio Elorza, *La razón y la sombra. Una lectura política de Ortega y Gasset* (Barcelona: Editorial Anagrama, 1984), 150.

105. Antonio Machado, "A orillas del Duero," *Poesías completas* (Madrid: Espasa-Calpe, 1965), 115.

106. An even measure of their romantic nationalism is provided by Antonio García Berrio: "As has often been said, the 1898ers view of Castile is similar to evocative romantic contemplation. . . . That is, the sentimental, ideological base controlling Machado's expressiveness in [*Campos de Castilla*], shares with romantic sentimentality both the rejection of an uninteresting present, or of a frankly miserable one according to circumstances, and the resulting flight into the historical or mythical past. (*Teoría de la literatura [La construcción del significado poético]* Segunda edición revisada y ampliada [Madrid: Cátedra, 1994], 175–176).

107. What does it reveal about the "liberal" (dis)interpretation of Carlism that there were not just Basque and Catalán but also Aragonese, Valencian, Galician, Andalusian, and Cantabrian Carlists? Certainly it says something important about those "Spaniards" known as "las masas campesinas," who were not attracted to the programs of either the supposed liberal revolutionaries or the reactionary absolutists. On Carlism and the masses, see Vicente Fernández Benítez's *Carlismo y rebeldía campesina* (Madrid: Siglo XXI, 1988).

108. García de Cortázar and J. M. González Vega, *Breve Historia de España* (Madrid: Alianza Editorial, 1994), 48. It is significant that Azorín was from Alicante, Blasco-Ibañez from Valencia, and Unamuno, Maeztu, and Baroja Castilian-speaking urban middle-class Basques from Bilbao and San Sebastián.

109. According to Herr, Sir Raymond Carr blames the political inefficiency on Spain's economic backwardness, which caused conflicts

between local and national interests. See Richard Herr, "La inestabilidad política de la España moderna," *Revista de Occidente* 107 (February 1972): 296. Herr's explanation centers on a slightly different "disyuntiva rural-urbana" (296–311).

110. "The Restoration, which came to power by force of arms— 'because such events are so common, History should ignore them,' Pérez Galdós has Mariclío say in the last of his *Episodios Nacionales*—used that force of arms to keep it in power and to defend it against the groups defeated in 1874 or in 1876, at the end of the Second Carlist War (1872–1876), or against the repeated actions of the Anarchists, which were especially threatening beginning in the 90s" (Jordi Canal, "Republicanos y carlistas contra el Estado: Violencia política en la España finisecular" in *Violencia y política en España*, ed. Julio Arostegui [Madrid: Marcial Pons, 1994], 57–58).

111. Valdés, *Rey, cortes y fuerza armada*, 486–487 (italics in original; my translation).

112. Diego López Garrido, *La Guardia Civil y los orígenes del estado centralista* (Barcelona: Editorial Crítica, 1982), 71. See also Manuel Ballbé, *Orden público y militarismo en la España constitutional (1812–1983)* (Madrid: Alianza Editorial, 1983), 141–154.

113. Of the two decades prior to the Republic, they add: "Militarism infused Spanish society, with its contempt for the rules of politics and its even more dangerous belief in the unity of the fatherland, which was in flat contradiction to the aspirations to autonomy of the Catalán bourgeoisie and the Basque Mesocracy. Thus the army became the keystone of a new kind of *Spanish nationalism*, whose ranks were joined by the Madrid bureaucracy, the mega-landowners in the South, by Church traditionalism, and by the Basque haute bourgeoisie, fearful of labor unrest and the inroads made by the slogans of Sabino Arana [founder of the Basque National Party]. Nothing could have been more tragic for Spain than the '*Spain-centrism*' ('españolismo') of these *patriots*, jingoist as in the Golden Age and anti-Enlightenment with the reactionaries of the XVIII-century" (de Cortázar and González Vega, *Breve Historia*, 48–49).

114. As the perspicacious Orwell remarked, "A government which sends boys of fifteen to the front with rifles forty years old and keeps its biggest men and newest weapons in the rear is manifestly more afraid of the revolution than of the fascists" (quoted from Noam Chomsky,

"Objectivity and Liberal Scholarship," in his *American Power and the New Mandarins: Historical and Political Essays* [New York: Pantheon Books, 1967], 102. I find Chomsky's critique of Gabriel Jackson's book on the Spanish Republic and the Civil War completely convincing).

115. Ernest Gellner, *Nations and Nationalism* (London: Routledge, 1983), 57.

116. Juan Linz, "Early State-Building and Late Peripheral Nationalisms against the State," in *Building States and Nations*, vol. 2, ed. S. N. Eisenstadt and S. Rokkan (Beverly Hills, Calif.: Sage, 1973, 33.

117. *España invertebrada* [1922] (Madrid: Alianza Editorial, 1983), 39. Although Ortega professes not to believe in the Reconquest, his explanation of Spain's "embriogenia defectuosa"(105), that Visigoths and not Franks were the origins of its feudalism, relies on the "Neo-Visigothic" premise that the Asturian-Leonese kings *were* lineal descendants of Visigothic royalty.

Chapter 2

1. Paul de Man, *The Rhetoric of Romanticism* (New York: Columbia University Press, 1984), 50, hereafter *RR*. Cynthia Chase glosses De Man's formulation as follows: "Our relation to Romanticism is being defined here as the interruption or absence of interpretation, and further as the interrupting or the disappearance of thematization. . . . In these terms it could be said that romantic literature *thematizes* the *disjunction* between [act and interpretation]" ("Translating Romanticism: Literary Theory As the Criticism of Aesthetics in the Work of Paul de Man," *Textual Practice* 4 [1990]: 352–353).

2. Christopher Fynsk, *Heidegger: Thought and Historicity* (Ithaca, N.Y.: Cornell University Press, 1986), 179–183, 185. The expression as employed here first appears in the Dilthey-Yorck correspondence. Thus: "Historicality is not world history but rather *being*-historical." See Theodore Kisiel, *The Genesis of Heidegger's "Being and Time* (Berkeley: University of California Press, 1995), 323.

3. The best interpreters—scholars, historians, or poets—are those who assume an adequate hermeneutical attitude to their past. This is because: "To be properly historical is not to make present but to be futural, which, with regard to the past to be disclosed, has brought itself into a

readiness to take the initiative, to take exception, even to give and take offense. The futurity of historical knowing thus becomes a critique of the present" (Kisiel, *Genesis of Heidegger's "Being and Time,"* 352).

4. Walter Benjamin, *Le concept de critique esthétique dans le romanticisme allemand,* trans. Philippe Lacoue-Labarthe and Anne-Marie Lang (Sainte-Amand [Cher.]: Flammarion, 1986), 37–38, note 3.

5. Rodolphe Gaché, "The Sober Absolute: On Benjamin and the Early Romantics," *SiR,* 31 (1992), 433.

6. L. Villacañas, *La quiebra de la razón ilustrada: Idealismo y romanticism* (Madrid: Editorial Cincel, 1988), 199–200.

7. This section follows Leonard P. Wessell, Jr.'s "Schiller and the Genesis of German Romanticism," *Studies in Romanticism* 10 (1971): 182–187, hereafter *SiR*.

8. Wessell, "Schiller and the Genesis of German Romanticism," 184.

9. Cited in ibid., 185.

10. Ibid., 187.

11. Ibid., 190.

12. Ibid., 191.

13. Ibid., 196.

14. Cited in Leonard P. Wessell, Jr., "The Antinomic Structure of Friedrich Schlegel's 'Romanticism'," *SiR* 12 (1973), 669.

15. Villacañas, *La quiebra de la razón ilustrada,* 204.

16. Philippe Lacoue-Labarthe and Jean-Luc Nancy, *L'absolue littéraire: Théorie de la littérature du romantisme allemand* (Paris: Editions du Seuil, 1978).

17. Lacoue-Labarthe and Nancy, *L'absolue littéraire,* quoted from *The Literary Absolute,* trans. Philip Barnard and Cheryl Lester (Albany: State University of New York Press, 1988), 12.

18. Ibid., 29.

19. Ibid., 33.

20. Ibid., 34–35.

21. Ibid., 35.

22. Ibid., "Translators' Introduction," xv.

23. Rodolphe Gaché, in "In-Difference to Philiosopy: de Man on Kant, Hegel, and Nietzsche," recalls de Man's appeal to a tradition of "romantic linguistics" (in *Reading de Man Reading,* ed. Lindsay Waters and Wlad Godzich (Minneapolis: University of Minnesota Press, 1989),

263, 287, 291. See also Paul de Man, *Allegories of Reading* (New Haven, Conn.: Yale University Press, 1979), 106, 130.

24. On theorizing romanticism—and the *of/about* distinction—see Herbert Lindenberger, *The History in Literature: On Value, Genre, Institutions* (New York: Columbia University Press, 1990), 61–84; and David Perkins, *Is Literary History Possible?* (Johns Hopkins University Press, 1993), chapter 5.

25. Just as there are echoes of Friedrich Schlegel's "Talk (*Gespräch*) on Poetry" (1800) in Bécquer's poetics.

26. See Janet Todd, *Sensibility: An Introduction* (New York: Methuen, 1986).

27. Marshall Brown, *Preromanticism* (Stanford, Calif.: Stanford University Press, 1991), 2 (my italics).

28. See Robert Marrast, *José de Espronceda y su tiempo*, tr. Laura Roca (Barcelona: Editorial Crítica, 1989), 59–61. My account of the assimilation of European aesthetics by Spanish Enlightenment figures draws heavily on Marrast.

29. Albert Derozier, "La ideología burguesa y los orígines de la novela histórica" in *Historia de España, VII (centralismo, ilustración, y agonía del antiguo régimen)*, ed. Fernando de Pinedo, Gil Novales, A. Derozier (Madrid: Editorial Labor, 1990), 406.

30. Marrast says: "It is easy to understand why, during his emigration, neither contemporary English nor French poets had any immediate or decisive effect on Espronceda's work, when we realize that it was not until then that he discovered Ossian, about forty years behind the times" (*José de Espronceda*, 188).

31. Derozier, "La ideología burguesa," 390.

32. See Marrast, *José de Espronceda*, 57–61.

33. The direct influence of Heine's criticism on Larra, Espronceda, and of his poetry on Bécquer, is another matter.

34. See Marrast, *José de Espronceda*, 361–372. Initially, neither Rivas's poetry nor Alcalá Galiano's Preface was much remarked, since they were so close to the "nationalistic" direction already prescribed by Durán (370).

35. For a revisionary view of the Espronceda-Teresa Mancha affair see Rosa Chacel's "Advertencia" to *Teresa* 3d ed. (Barcelona: Editorial Bruguera, 1983). Her fictional recreation is based on Cascales Muñoz's *El*

auténtico Espronceda pornográfico y el apócrifo en general and conversations with Cascales himself.

36. For details see Marrast, *José de Espronceda*, 92–102, 178–187, 408–409.

37. W. T. Pattison says in reference to Espronceda's years abroad, "Undoubtedly Espronceda was then much more occupied with political schemes, revolutionary movements, and especially his affair with Teresa than with the new literature" (cited in Marrast, 218). Although Marrast finds Pattison too harsh, he seems to agree. While Espronceda's comrades in exile in Paris—Hernáiz, Cortés, Bernabeu, Ochoa, Alvear, Juanicó, Madrazo—were working and studying, he lived first on subsistence money paid Spanish liberal exiles by the French government, and later on money sent from Madrid by his parents. As Marrast remarks, "The only activity we can be certain—thanks to the police spies—occupied Espronceda's time, aside from poetry, was fencing" (176).

38. Marrast, *José de Espronceda*, 219.

39. Marrast, *José de Espronceda*, 189.

40. Marrast observes of an autograph essay by Espronceda (1828–1830), comparing Tasso and Voltaire, that like Lista his teacher, and for the same reasons, the younger poet much preferred Tasso: "[Lista] always insisted on the requirement of harmony between content and form, on the choice of a poetic expressiveness adjusted to the ideas, the sentiments and the descriptions, as well as on the need to vary registers according to the different parts of a long composition, or according to the genre of shorter works" (*José de Espronceda*, 183).

41. Marrast, *José de Espronceda*, 362.

42. Derek Flitter, *Spanish Romantic Literary Theory and Criticism* (Cambridge: Cambridge University Press, 1992), 100–101.

43. See Javier Herrero, "El naranjo romántico: Esencia del costumbrismo," *Hispanic Review* 2 (1978): 343–354.

44. Hans Juretschke, *Origen doctrinal y génesis del romanticismo español* (Madrid: Ateneo, 1954), 34.

45. Ibid., 37–38.

46. Flitter, *Spanish Romantic Literary Theory*, 185.

47. Rubén Benítez, "Introducción" to Gustavo Adolfo Bécquer, *Rimas. Leyendas escogidas* (Madrid: Taurus, 1990), 21–22.

48. Thomas Weiskel, *The Romantic Sublime: Studies in the Structure*

and Psychology of Transcendence (Johns Hopkins University Press, 1976), 26.

49. See the virtuoso proleptic entombment passage of Carta 3 (*Desde mi celda*), in which Bécquer ranks poetry's historical importance and regenerative power above historical action. An early critic who draws attention to the importance of Bécquer's prose is Arturo Berenguer Carisomo, *La prosa de Bécquer* [1947] Segunda edición corregida y aumentada (Seville: Publicaciones de la Universidad de Sevilla, 1974), who advises, "I wish to demonstrate, by the time this essay is finished, that the best of Bécquer is his prose; I am tempted to say, if it didn't sound like heresy, that it is superior to his verse" (2).

50. Søren Kierkegaard, *Fear and Trembling / Repetition*, ed. and trans. Howard V. Hong and Edna H. Hong (Princeton, N.J.: Princeton University Press, 1983), 131.

51. Jerome J. McGann, *The Romantic Ideology: A Critical Investigation* (University of Chicago Press, 1983), 27; J. Hillis Miller, "Tradition and Difference," *Diacritics* 2 (1972): 7–13; Virgil Nemoianu, *The Taming of Romanticism: European Literature and the Age of Biedermeier* (Cambridge, Mass.: Harvard University Press, 1984), 36.

52. Paul de Man, *Blindness and Insight: Essays in the Rhetoric of Contemporary Criticism*, 2d edition (University of Minnesota Press, 1983), 165, hereafter *BI2*.

53. Cited in Suzanne Gearhart, "Philosophy *Before* Literature: Deconstruction, Historicity, and the Work of Paul de Man," *Diacritics* 13 (Winter 1983): 72.

54. Paul de Man, *RR*, 10.

55. Meyer H. Abrams, *Natural Supernaturalism: Tradition and Revolution in Romantic Literature* [1971] (New York: Norton, 1973), 95–96.

56. Geoffrey Hartman and Harold Bloom significantly increased the degree of subjective autonomy in the Wellek-Abrams subject-object paradigm, the former by emphasizing temporality and the latter by a diachronic rhetorical emphasis. See Thomas Pfau, "Rhetorical and Existential: Romantic Studies and the Question of the Subject," *SiR* 26 (1978): 487–512.

57. De Man, *BI2*, xii. The essay itself was first published in *Interpretation*, ed. Charles Singleton (Johns Hopkins University Press,

1969). Wlad Godzich remembers Jonathan Culler remarking that it was "the most photocopied essay in literary criticism" (*BI2*, xvi).

58. Quoted by de Man on p. 206.

59. On the French Hegelian scene, see Judith P. Butler, *Subjects of Desire* (New York: Columbia University Press, 1987). If he had remained in Europe, Paul de Man would have written a dissertation on Hegel and Hölderlin. Instead he wrote the dissertation "Mallarmé, Yeats and the Post-Romantic Predicament" (Harvard University, May 1960). Its original title was "Poetic Mediation in Mallarmé, [Stefan] George, and Yeats."

60. Between 1936 and 1951 Heidegger wrote five essays related to his reading of Hölderlin's poetry and prose.

61. De Man, *BI2*, 241–242, italics in original.

62. See Philippe Lacoue-Labarthe, "Hölderlin and the Greeks," *Typology: Mimesis, Philosophy, Politics* (Cambridge, Mass.: Harvard University Press, 1989), 237–238, 240.

63. De Man, *RR*, 294, note 23.

64. See "Heidegger's Exegeses of Hölderlin," [1955] *BI2*, 246, note 1.

65. De Man, *BI2*, 259.

66. Lacoue-Labarthe, *Typography*, 242–243.

67. Friedrich Hölderlin, *Essays and Letters*, trans. and ed. Thomas Pfau (Albany: State University of New York Press, 1988), 149.

68. For Heidegger, authentic Dasein is not *in* history, it is literally the (as with Hölderlin, at times *poetic*) making *of* history.

69. Paul de Man, *Critical Writings, 1953–1978*, ed. Lindsay Waters (Minneapolis: University of Minnesota Press, 1989), 72–73, hereafter *CW*. See Martin Heidegger, *Being and Time*, trans. John Macquarrie and Edward Robinson (New York: Harper & Row, 1962), section 75, 443.

70. Heidegger, *Being and Time*, 440–441.

71. De Man, *RR*, 15.

72. De Man, *RR*, 14.

73. On the joining of these two terms see chapter 5 below.

74. De Man, *CW*, 32–33 (italics are mine.) The "divided character of our being" recalls Hölderlin's contestation of Schiller and Fichte in favor—writes Bodei—of discovering "unity, absolute being, only in the separation of its parts, and in the heart of multiplicity itself. Totality shines forth, therefore, only in these divisions" (Remei Bodei, *Hölderlin:*

La filosofía y lo trágico [1980], trans. Díaz de Atauri [Madrid: Visor, 1990], 26–27). Cf. de Man's remark, "For poetry, the divide exists forever," in the early essay "The Dead-End of Formalist Criticism" (1956), *BI2*, 240. On this point Heidegger and de Man follow Hölderlin. As Fynsk observes, "Indeed, in his lectures of 1934–1935, Heidegger calls the task of holding the separation between gods and man, between the earth and what Hölderlin calls 'the savage world of the dead,' the essence of the poetic, founding project of historical Dasein. In the fundamental tonality of mourning—which is the essence of the tragic experience—the poet occupies and founds the *Mitte des Seins*. This latter, Heidegger suggests, is to be understood in relation to the ontological difference" (Fynsk, *Heidegger*, 183).

75. Bodei, *Hölderlin*, 66–67.

76. Hölderlin, *Essays*, 97.

77. De Man, *RR*, 41.

78. De Man, *CW*, 74.

79. Cited in Suzanne R. Kirschner, *The Religious and Romantic Origins of Psychoanalysis: Individuation and Integration in Post-Freudian Theory* (Cambridge: Cambridge University Press, 1996).

80. It might perhaps be argued that my counter-theory is a surreptitious *synthesis* of all four.

81. See Juan Luis Alborg, *Historia de la literatura española*. Vol. 4, *El Romanticismo* (Madrid: Gredos, 1980), for a thorough bibliography on the various theories of Spanish romanticism down to 1980; see especially the footnotes to chapter 1. For a more recent comprehensive bibliography on all aspects of Spanish romanticism see Leonardo Romero Tobar, *Panorama crítico del romanticismo español* (Madrid: Editorial Castalia, 1994).

82. Cited in Alborg, *Historia,* 4:37–38.

83. Ibid., 50.

84. In fairness to Alborg, he will complete his treatment of the problem of romanticism in a second volume.

85. Alborg, *Historia,* 4:69.

86. Octavio Paz, *Los hijos del limo: Del romanticismo a la vanguardia* [1972; 1974], 3d edition (Barcelona: Seix Barral, 1981).

87. Paz, *Los hijos del limo,* 128.

88. Nemoianu, *The Taming of Romanticism*, 37–39.

89. See Vicente's Llorens' remark, chapter 1, note 73, supra.

90. It is a nice irony that "Pablo Neruda" is a penname, apparently borrowed from the Czech Biedermeier short-story writer, Jan Neruda.

91. My thesis subsumes José Angel Valente's contention in "Luis Cernuda y la poesía de la meditación [1959]," *Las palabras de la tribu* (Madrid: Siglo XXI, 1971), 127–143. Antonio García Berrio clarifies Valente's point when he says that Cernuda revives the practice of a "discursive poetry," in *Teoría de la literatura* (Madrid: Cátedra, 1994).

Chapter 3

1. Rubén Benítez, *Bécquer tradicionalista* (Madrid: Gredos, 1971); Robert Pageard, *Bécquer: leyenda y realidad*, ed. Hans Juretschke (Madrid: Espasa-Calpe, 1990).

2. Benítez, *Bécquer*, 23–28.

3. Bécquer is indebted to Pablo Piferrer's *Recuerdos y bellezas de España* project, itself inspired by the *Romancero* and by Chateaubriand's *Les Aventures du dernier Abencérrage* (see Derek Flitter, *Spanish Romantic Literary Theory and Criticism* [Cambridge: Cambridge University Press, 1992], 100–101.)

4. Chateaubriand, *Los mártires: El triunfo de la religión cristiana*, trans. Manuel M. Flamant (Madrid: Imprenta de Gaspar y Roig, 1852), 136.

5. Benítez, *Bécquer*, 51.

6. Gustavo Adolfo Bécquer, *Obras completas*, 8th edition (Madrid: Aguilar, 1954), 833.

7. Quoted in Benítez, *Bécquer*, 52 ("inapreciables testimonios").

8. Ibid., 54–55.

9. Cited by Ramírez Araújo in his outstanding "Bécquer y la reconstrucción del pasado" in *Gustavo Adolfo Bécquer*, ed. Russell P. Sebold, 8th edition (Madrid: Taurus, 1982), 253. (Unless otherwise noted the pagination in parentheses refers to Gustavo Adolfo Bécquer, *Obras completas* (Madrid: Aguilar, 1954.)

10. Benítez, *Bécquer*, 55–56 (italics mine).

11. The expression is the translators'. See Martin Heidegger, *Being and Time*, trans. by John Macquarrie and Edward Robinson (New York:

Harper & Row, 1962), 438, note 1. What is at issue in Bécquer, then, is not "a merely mechanical repetition or an attempt to reconstitute the physical past; it means rather an attempt to go back to the past and retrieve former *possibilities*, which are thus 'explicitly handed down' or 'transmitted' (437, note 1). Here is Heidegger on this "conversation": "The repeating of that which is possible does not bring again [Wiederbringen] something that is 'past,' nor does it bind the 'Present' back to that which has already been 'outstripped.' Arising, as it does, from a resolute projection of oneself, repetition does not let itself be per-suaded of something by what is 'past,' just in order that this, as some-thing which was formerly actual, may recur. Rather, the repetition makes a *reciprocative rejoinder* to the possibility of that existence which has-been-there. But when such a rejoinder is made to this possibility in a resolution, it is made *in a moment of vision; and as such* it is at the same time a *disavowal* of that which in the 'today,' is working itself out as the 'past'" (437–438). I return to this concept in chapter 5.

12. Cited in Louis Wirth Marvick, *Mallarmé and the Sublime* (Albany: State University of New York Press, 1986), 185, note 8.

13. As Ramírez Araújo remarks, in *Gustavo Adolfo Bécquer* (Madrid: Taurus, 1982), 252. The Picturesque *does* appear in the *Cartas desde mi celda* and in the *Leyendas*.

14. See Alfonso Botti's study of National Catholicism (*Cielo y dinero: El nacionalcatolicismo en España (1881–1975)* [1992] (Madrid: Alianza Editorial, 1992), which begins with the *Manifiesto de los persas* (1814).

15. For an especially convincing explanation of Bécquer's proto-sym-bolism, see María Angeles Naval, *El sentimiento apócrifo (Un estudio del cantar literario en Aragón, 1880–1900)* (Zaragoza: Institución Fernando el Católico, 1990), 113–139.

16. See Hans Juretschke, *Vida, obra y pensamiento de Alberto Lista* (Madrid: C.S.I.C., 1951), 419–465; and María del Carmen García Tejera, *Conceptos y teorías literarias españolas del siglo XIX: Alberto Lista* (Cádiz: Servicio de Publicaciones de la Universidad de Cádiz, 1989), which contains ten Lista texts from *Ensayos literarios y críticos por D. Alberto Lista y Aragón* (2 vols.) recopilados y prologados por José Joaquín de Mora (Seville, 1844).

17. I have found one reference to the figure of personification in

Bécquer—in Francisco López Estrada's *Poética para un poeta: Las "Cartas literarias a una mujer" de Bécquer* (Madrid: Gredos, 1972), 159.

18. Benítez, *Bécquer*, 60. ("Las técnicas descriptivas del tradicionalismo artístico se advierten con mayor claridad en la *Historia de los templos*, pero persisten en el resto de la obra de Bécquer; no sólo en sus notas sobre monumentos, sino también en las leyendas y en las *Rimas*.")

19. Munárriz in translating Addison gives "mind" as "ánimo"; for his Spanish contemporaries "ánimo," "entendimiento," and even "mente," were part of the soul and not of the brain. Clearly they preferred the psychology of St. Agustine to that of Locke and Addison. See the prefatory study by Tonia Raquejo, the modern Spanish editor of Joseph Addison, *Los placeres de la imaginación y otros ensayos de The Spectator* (Madrid: Visor, 1991), 129–130, note.

20. García Tejera, *Conceptos y Teoría*, 144.

21. Geoffrey Hartman, "'Was it for this. . . ?': Wordsworth and the Birth of the Gods," in *Romantic Revolutions: Criticism and Theory*, ed. Kenneth R. Johnston et. al. (Bloomington: Indiana University Press, 1990), 10.

22. Martin Price, "The Sublime Poem: Pictures and Powers," in *Poets of Sensibility and the Sublime*, ed. by Harold Bloom (New York: Chelsea House, 1986), 36. Bécquer speaks disapprovingly of the "delirio de regeneración clásica" of the Spanish Renaissance (*OC*, 898).

23. On Espronceda's poetic epistemology, and his *implicit* "creative perception" recall from *El diablo mundo*: "Y les [los verdes prados] presta su alma su hermosura, / Y el corazón su amor y lozanía, / Su mente les regala su frescura, / Y su rico color su fantasía. . . " (*El estudiante de Salamanca / El diablo mundo*, ed. Robert Marrast [Madrid: Castalia, 1982], 271).

24. Benítez, *Bécquer*, 71–72. It is virtually impossible to encounter the *Historia* in unmutilated form.

25. Ibid., 77. R. Pageard also says, "Bécquer then lists the different fields of specialization with an intelligent series of resounding epic images that seem to me forced: he has the architects leave their tombs. . . " (*Bécquer*, 205).

26. Angela Leighton, *Shelley and the Sublime: An Interpretation of the Major Poems* (New York: Cambridge University Press), 21.

27. Marvick, *Mallarmé and the Sublime*, 79–80.

28. ("reducir vuestra majestad a líneas"—"recuerdos a números"—
"la melancolía que sueña en vuestro seno me envuelva entre sus alas
transparentes," 897).

29. García Tejera, *Conceptos y Teoría*, 162–164.

30. Romantic historians never failed to point out parallels between
the lives and fortunes of Isabel I and Isabel II (Queen of Spain from
1833–1868).

31. Instances of hypotyposis, descriptive and rhetorical, are thus the
rhetorical markers of Bécquer's national-romantic sublime. See Bernard
Dupriez, *Gradus: Les procédés littéraires (Dictionnaire)* (Paris: Christian
Bourgois Éditeur, 1984), 240.

32. Martin Price, "The Sublime Poem," 44.

33. ("¡Atrás!, ¡atrás! Los ojos se ciegan, una nube de cenizas
calientes y de espeso humo cubre como un velo funeral este cuadro
espantoso" 904). There are other curious examples of this from
within/from without narration in his prose, each perhaps suggesting the
juncture at which, according to Paul de Man, "reading might begin";
that is, where rhetoric and thematics start to interfere with one another.
For a cogent "positivization" of de Man's declarations about the absolute
limits that rhetorical figures place on expressiveness, see Antonio García
Berrio, *Teoría de la literatura (La construcción del significado poético)*
Segunda edición revisada y ampliada (Madrid: Ediciones Cátedra, 1994),
367–370.

34. Mª del C. García Tejera, *Conceptos y teorías* 102–103. There is no
question of Bécquer's familiarity with Lista's lectures. In l. 50 of his allegorical "A Quintana (Fantasía)" (1854–1855), Bécquer uses the same line
from Racine that Lista used to exemplify a sublime verse: "Celui qui met
un frein à la fureur des flots." The origin of Racine's verse is Job, 38:11.

35. Lista seems typical in this regard. According to María Angeles
Naval, the early nineteenth-century "preceptistas"—Alvarez Giménez,
Bellido González—held that the sublime appeared in Nature, but that
literary description was its vehicle. The sublime was usually considered a
superior degree of beauty; also, the transcription of sublime experience
called for a "forma concisa, breve y enérgica," rather than "un estilo
ampuloso, rico en imágenes." Fundamental, according to Professor
Naval, was "the importance of the moral sublime and within this of its
religious, Christian elements to which the sublime is conducive" (María

Angeles Naval, *Luis Ram de Viu, 1864–1906. Vida y Obra. Un poeta de la Restauración* [Zaragoza: Instituto de Fernando el Católico, 1995], 188.).

36. Cited in Antonio Carrillo Alonso, G. A. *Bécquer y los cantares de Andalucía* (Madrid: Fundación Universitaria Española, 1991), 83. A. Berenguer Carisomo reports that Cossío too said that in the *Rimas* "había mucho cante jondo" (*La prosa de Bécquer* [Sevilla: Universidad de Sevilla, 1974], 60).

37. Carlos Bousoño, "Los conjuntos paralelísticos de Bécquer" [1951], in Sebold, ed., *Gustavo Adolfo Bécquer*, 157–190.

38. Lista wrote, for example: "—Tiende noche benigna / tu oscuro velo, / que me importa la vida / ver a mi dueño; / y amor me dice / que tu sombra y tu venda / me harán felice" (cited in Antonio Carrillo Alonso, G. A. *Bécquer y los cantares de Andalucía* (Madrid: Fundación Universitaria Española, 1991), 96.

39. David Walker, *The Transparent Lyric: Reading and Meaning in the Poetry of Stevens and Williams* (Princeton University Press, 1984), 10

40. Here personification serves as proto-imagination, imaging "creatures" no longer found in the natural world. In *Pleasures of the Imagination*, Addison exclaimed (Munárriz trans.): "quántos caminos tiene la poesía para dirigirse a la imaginación, como que no está limitada á solo la naturaleza, sino que crea mundos nuevos, nos muestra personas que no se hallan en parte alguna, y aun representa las facultades del alma . . . en forma y carácter sensibles" (Addison, *Los placeres de la imaginación*, 201–202).

41. José Pedro Díaz, *Gustavo Adolfo Bécquer: Vida y obra* 3d edition corrected and amplified (Madrid: Gredos, 1971), 234.

42. Cited in Gustavo Adolfo Bécquer, *Rimas*, ed. José Carlos de Torres (Madrid: Castalia, 1984), 44, note 38 ("de la égloga, la sencillez; de la leyenda, el calor; de los romances antiguos, la melancolía, y de los cantos populares, el espíritu").

43. See García Tejera, *Conceptos y teorías*, 102, 105.

44. Luis Lavaur, *Teoría romántica del cante jondo* (Madrid: Editora Nacional, 1976) 94–95. It seems that the notion of "Middle Eastern" Flamenco songs is also a romantic invention; the first famous "cantaor" was Silverio Franconetti (1831–1893), the son of an Italian opera singer, who modeled the first Tablado Flamenco in Seville on the Parisian "café chantant." So much for the timeless oriental roots of this cornerstone of topical *españolismo*.

45. The Vulgate reads "*super flumina Babylonis. . . .*"

46. Recall Longinus's example of extreme brevity: the "Fiat lux" example, copied by both Blair and Lista.

47. The "X" represents the delayed subject of the verbs "passed" and "had" (*ha pasado*) (*llevaba*), which is not revealed until the fourth verse, precipitating the sublime effect. Ferrán's version retained the pathetic diminutives—"carrito" and "manita"—of traditional versions.

48. This "Rima" appeared as no. 11 in the *Libro de los gorriones*, the only known ordering of the "Rimas" by the poet himself.

49. ("that is natural [a Lista criterion], brief, [and] crisp, that leaps from the soul like an electric spark, that wounds [our non-sensual capacity for] feeling with a [single] word and dashes off, and naked of artifice, easy within a free form, in touching but one, awakens a thousand ideas that sleep in the bottomless ocean of fantasy." 1297).

50. In "A Sketch," as in Rima 34, a woman (Julia) passes for a human manifestation of—or in harmony with—sublime nature, until she speaks, which her mother had forbidden her to do before eligible bachelors.

51. ("The true hymn, the poetic word made flesh, was that silent, immobile woman whose glance was never caught by any chance obstacle, whose thoughts could never be contained by any form, whose pupils encompassed the entire horizon, absorbing all its light and reflecting it back again. Until I saw them together, I never completely realized the majesty of these three immensities: the sea, the sky and Julia's bottomless pupils. Scenes ["imágenes"] so gigantic that only those eyes could copy them" [773]).

52. This forestalled the development of the Great Romantic Lyric in Spain. See on this fundamental point Leonardo Romero Tobar, *Panorama crítico del romanticismo español* (Madrid: Editorial Castalia, 1994), 228.

53. See Gustavo Adolfo Bécquer, *Rimas*, ed. Russell P. Sebold (Madrid: Espasa-Calpe, 1991), 82–83.

Chapter 4

1. Deborah Esch, "A Defence of Rhetoric / The Triumph of Reading," in *Reading De Man Reading*, ed. Lindsay Waters and W.

Godzich (Minneapolis: University of Minnesota Press, 1989), 74.

2. Study of the Esproncedan sublime would confirm that what critics describe as "metaphysical anguish" was accepted by a contemporary critic (Enrique Gil y Carrasco) as perfectly understandable, if undesirable, given the chaotic social and political situation caused by the "siglo filosófico" and the French Revolution. See Derek Flitter, *Spanish Romantic Literary Theory and Criticism* (Cambridge: Cambridge University Press, 1992), 117–118.

3. Luis Cernuda, *Prosa I: Obra completa II*, ed. by Derek Harris and Luis Maristany (Madrid: Ediciones Siruela, 1994), 80–81. Subsequent references, with "book" and page are to the Siruela edition.

4. The same restitutive romanticism appears in Catalunya via Joan Maragall's fascination with Goethe and Heine.

5. Luis Cernuda, *Poesía completa: Obra completa, I*, ed. by Derek Harris and Luis Maristany (Madrid: Ediciones Siruela, 1993), 614–615. "Written on Water" was the final poem in the first edition of *Ocnos* (London: Dolphin, 1942).

6. "Primordial concern" translates the concept of "tema vital" as formulated by Pedro Salinas in *La poesía de Rubén Darío* (Buenos Aires: Losada, 1948), 48.

7. Walter Terence Stace, *Time and Eterniy: An Essay in the Philosophy of Religion* (Princeton, N.J.: Princeton University Press, 1952), 76.

8. Ashton Nichols, *The Poetics of Epiphany: Nineteenth-Century Origins of the Modern Literary Movement* (University of Alabama Press, 1987), chapter 2.

9. See W. P. Albrecht, "The Tragic Sublime of Hazlitt and Keats," *Studies in Romanticism* 20 (Summer 1981): 185–201. See also my "Pedro Salinas y lo sublime romántico," in *Signo y memoria de Pedro Salinas*, ed. de Enric Bou and Elena Gascón Vera (Madrid: Editorial Pliegos, 1993), 97–105.

10. Cernuda, *Prosa I*, 604.

11. Here is the basis for a comparison with the solipsistic gesture of Espronceda in "Canto a Teresa" (stanza 16), in which Espronceda seems close to Coleridge (in "Dejection: An Ode [Stanza 4]). However, the latter is able to fall back on the esemplastic power of the romantic

Imagination and on the "wedding [of] Nature to us" (stanza 5), which Espronceda and Cernuda, for different reasons, cannot do.

12. On the Spanish side this "Platonic"—but phenomenologically driven—"saving of appearances" was stressed by Ortega y Gasset in *Meditaciones del Quijote* (1914).

13. Octavio Paz, "La palabra edificante (Luis Cernuda)" in *Cuadrivio* (México City: Joaquín Mortiz, 1965), 167–203.

14. See M. H. Abrams, *Natual Supernaturalism: Tradition and Revolution in Romantic Literature* (Norton, 1973), 380–384.

15. At the same time the third, or "wedding," stage in Abrams's paradigm may appear in Cernuda when he becomes aware of the "intimations of immortality" in his pursuit of his own youth through the Other.

16. Cernuda, *Poesía I, Ocnos,* 595.

17. Cernuda, *Poesía I, Los placeres prohibidos,* 177.

18. Cernuda, *Poesía I, Variaciones,* 648–649.

19. Cernuda, *Prosa I, Estudios sobre poesía española,* 111.

20. Cernuda, *Poesía I, Ocnos,* 614. Instead of saying "I" in his prose poems Cernuda often uses the familiar, second-person address, "tú."

21. Luis Antonio de Villena, "Cernuda recordado por Aleixandre (Notas de vida y literatura)," in *A una verdad: Luis Cernuda (1902–1963),* ed. Andrés Trapiello and Juan Manuel Bonet (Seville: Universidad Internacional Menéndez Pelayo, 1988), 82–91.

22. Cernuda, *Poesía I, La realidad y el deseo,* 217.

23. Luis Cernuda, *F. Hölderlin: Poemas* (Madrid: Visor, 1985), 17.

24. Cernuda, *Poesía I, La realidad y el deseo,* 222.

25. Cernuda, *Poesía I, La realidad y el deseo,* 311.

26. Antonio García Berrio, *Teoría de la literatura (La construcción del significado poético),* 2d edition (Madrid: Cátedra, 1994), 472.

27. Luis Antonio de Villena, ed. *Las Nubes / Desolación de la Quimera,* de Luis Cernuda (Madrid: Cátedra, 1984), 45–46. This discovery is a minor instance of "resolute repetition." The new generation needed Cernuda as a precursor of their own "culturalist" practice.

28. *Origine du Drame Baroque Allemand,* trans. Sibylle Muller, Preface by Irving Wohlfarth (Paris: Flammarion, 1985), 191.

29. Cernuda, *Prosa I,* "Palabras antes de una lectura," 601–606. Until recently, this talk was only available in this 1941 version, although it was first delivered in 1935. See Harris, ed., *Prosa I,* 45–49; P. W. Silver,

Luis Cernuda: El poeta en su leyenda [1965; 1972] (Madrid: Castalia, 1995), 67; Jenaro Talens (*El espacio y las máscaras: Introducción a la lectura de Luis Cernuda* [Barcelona: Anagrama, 1975]), 211–212.

30. Angela Leighton, *Shelley and the Sublime: An Interpretation of the Major Poems* (Cambridge: Cambridge University Press, 1984), 21.

31. Cernuda, *Poesía I, Ocnos*, 553 (italics mine).

32. Cernuda, *Poesía I, Ocnos* ("Belleza oculta"), 566 (italics mine).

33. Cernuda, *Prosa I*, "Palabras antes de una lectura," 603.

34. Hölderlin, *Poemas*, Introducción y versión de Luis Cernuda, 18.

35. Cernuda, *Prosa I*, 604–605.

36. The reader will notice here in the later Spanish poetic tradition the same absence of "internalization" observed in Espronceda and Bécquer. Hence the reference to "personification" as well as to allegory.

37. Cernuda lends particular emphasis to the incommensurability of the two. His divinities are allegorical "figures" that image this imbalance, or what Lacoue-Labarthe calls, "l'incommensurabilité du sensible au métaphysique (à l'Idée, à Dieu)," in "La vérité sublime," from *Du sublime*, ed. Jean-Luc Nancy (Alençon [Orne]: Éditions Belin, 1988), 122.

38. Carlos A. Disandro, "Hölderlin y el sentimiento de las ruinas," *Friedrich Hölderlin 1770–1970* (La Plata: Universidad de La Plata, 1971), 167–168.

39. Cernuda, Poesía I, *La realidad y el deseo*, 414.

40. Cernuda, *Prosa I*, ("Palabras antes de una lectura" [Primera versión, 1935]), 851.

41. Cernuda, *Prosa I*, 852. This talk was probably delivered in 1935 when the definitive title was chosen for the collected poems. The inception of "allegorism" in Cernuda is post-1942.

42. Antonio de Villena, ed., *Las Nubes*, 45, 46–48.

43. Bejamin, *Origine*, 197.

44. Benjamin, *Origine*, 244. There is a remarkable prescience also regarding allegory in Cernuda's use of the verse "Et in Arcadia Ego" (*Poesía I*, 538). He anticipates Panofsky's elucidation of the paired meanings—Eros-Thanatos—of this phrase in *Meaning in the Visual Arts*.

45. Cernuda, *Poesía I*, 553 (italics mine). Recall Bécquer's denunciation of the shortcomings of painterly contrast in Murillo.

46. Jean-François Lyotard, *La posmodernidad (explicada a los niños)*, trans. by Enrique Lynch (Barcelona: Gedisa, 1987), 20–21.

47. Lyotard, 25.

48. As Slavoj Zizek writes: "The Sublime is therefore the paradox of an object which, in the very field of representation, provides a view, in a negative way, of the dimension of what is unrepresentable." Cited in Vijay Mishra, *The Gothic Sublime* (Albany: State University of New York Press, 1994), 203.

49. Philippe Lacoue-Labarthe, *La Poésie comme Expérience* (Paris: Christian Bourgois Editeur, 1986), 128.

50. Lacoue-Labarthe, *La Poésie comme Expérience*, 128.

51. Cited in Lacoue-Labarthe, *La Poésie comme Expérience*, 98 (italics in original).

52. Cernuda, *Prosa I*, PL, 605–606.

Chapter 5

1. Friedrich Hölderlin, *Essays and Letters*, trans. and ed. Thomas Pfau (Albany: State University of New York Press, 1988), 150. Thomas Pfau explains (181) that the reference to Spain was Hölderlin's way of alluding to his own journey as far south as Bordeaux. A play by his correspondant, Böhlendorff, was *set* in Spain. I have based my *altered* version of Hölderlin's letter no. 240 on Pfau's translation of the original (152–153).

2. This section draws on Andrzej Warminski's "Monstrous History: Heidegger Reading Hölderlin," *Yale French Studies* 77 (1990): 193–209. If my account reads like parody I have failed to do justice to his profound essay.

3. Paul de Man, *Critical Writings, 1953–1978*, ed. Lindsay Waters (University of Minnesota Press, 1989), 73 (italics mine).

4. As Américo Castro wrote, "Pride, prejudices and a confused sense of values kept us from realizing that Spain was not entirely a Western country" (quoted in the Preface to Américo Castro, *Sobre el nombre y el quién de los españoles*, ed. Rafael Lapesa (Madrid: Taurus Ediciones, 1985), 12. See also Vicente Llorens, "La discontinuidad Española: La invasión árabe y el legado de la antigüedad clásica," *Revista de Occidente* 121 (April 1973): 3–23.

5. There is apparent leeway in de Man's accounts of Hölderlin's chiasmic figure. The explanation is that de Man intended the figure to apply to what he called the "post-romantic predicament." Thus he spoke of the

Greek's "native" as usurpation of the Gods'part and "sacred pathos" but also (as translated by Hölderlin to modern or romantic terms) as nostalgia for the ontological stability of the natural object. See, for example, Paul de Man, *Critical Writings, 1953–1978*, ed. Lindsay Waters (University of Minnesota Press, 1989), 74.

6. Anthony Pagden, *Spanish Imperialism and the Political Imagination: Studies in European and Spanish-American Social and Political Theory 1513–1830* (New Haven, Conn.: Yale University Press, 1990), 1–2.

7. Martin Heidegger, *Being and Time*, trans. John Macquarrie and Edward Robinson (New York: Harper & Row, 1962), 441.

8. Heidegger, *Being and Time*, 443–444.

9. Ibid., 437. The words "in the process of *having-been*" seem a close precursor of de Man's "slipping into the past."

10. Heidegger, *Being and Time*, 436.

11. Ibid., 436.

12. Ibid., 438, note 1.

13. This point gains support and in turn "updates" the eighteenth-century idea of genius, as defined by Kant, and is related to both Longinus's and Kant's notions of the sublime, as Lacoue-Labarthe shows in "La vérité sublime," (in *Du sublime*, ed. Jean-François Courtine et. al. [Alençon (Orne): Éditions Belin, 1988]) where he writes: "La transmission et la répétition du génie se fait donc par une sorte de (mystérieuse) contagion mimétique, mais qui n'est pas l'imitation. Comme tentera de l'expliquer Kant, des grandes oeuvres d'art il ne faut pas user comme de modèles d'une imitation (*Nachmachung*) mais comme de pièces ou d'éléments d'une succession ou d'un héritage (*Nachfolge*)," 139.

14. John Hollander, *The Figure of Echo: A Mode of Allusion in Milton and After* (Berkeley: University of California Press, 1981), 133, introduces *transumptio* in his discussion of Harold Bloom.

15. (My italics.) Christopher Fynsk, *Heidegger: Thought and Historicity* (Ithaca, N.Y.: Cornell University Press, 1986), 133. The idea of upstaging Bloom is Fynsk's. This seems another echo of Paul de Man's movement of "passing beyond" (see footnote 9).

16. Paul de Man, *The Rhetoric of Romanticism* (Columbia University Press, 1984), 50.

17. To use Christopher Fynsk's words as a gloss: "The originary encounter with itself and with the other, as the other, forms a kind of

temporal horizon for Dasein in both past and future; this encounter will have never taken place and will never take place—or it will have taken place, as Blanchot would put it, in an "immemorial past" and will come about in a future always still to come" (*Heidegger*, 51).

18. De Man, *Critical Writings*, 33. See also chapter 2, note 74, supra.

19. Warminski, "Monstrous History," 209.

SELECTED
BIBLIOGRAPHY

Abrams, M. H. *Natural Supernaturalism: Tradition and Revolution in Romantic Literature.* New York: Norton, 1973.

Alborg, Juan Luis. *Historia de la literatura española.* Vol 4, *El romanticismo.* Madrid: Gredos, 1980.

Aullón de Haro, Pedro. *La poesía del siglo XIX.* Madrid: Editorial Playor, 1982.

Ballbé, Manuel. *Orden público y militarismo en la España constitucional (1812–1983).* Madrid: Alianza Editorial, 1983.

Bécquer, Gustavo Adolfo. *Obras completas,* 8th edition. Madrid: Aguilar, 1954.

Benitez, Rubén. *Bécquer tradicionalista.* Madrid: Gredos, 1971.

Bernal, A.-M., B. Clavero, and E. Fernández de Pinedo, eds. *Antiguo Régimen y liberalismo: Homenaje a Miguel Artola, 1. Visiones Generales.* Madrid: Alianza Editorial/Ediciones de la Universidad Autónoma de Madrid, 1994.

Blanco Valdés, Roberto L. *Rey, Cortes y fuerza armada en los orígenes de la España liberal, 1808–1823.* Madrid: Siglo XIX, 1988.

Butler, Marilyn. *Romantics, Rebels and Reactionaries: English Literature and Its Background 1760–1830.* Oxford: Oxford University Press, 1981.

Cardwell, Richard A. "The Persistence of Romantic Thought in Spain," *Modern Language Review* 65 (1970): 803–812.

Cernuda, Luis. *Poesía completa: Obra completa I.* Edited by Derek Harris and Luis Maristany. Madrid: Ediciones Siruela, 1993.

———. *Prosa I: Obra completa II.* Edited by Derek Harris and Luis Maristany. Madrid: Ediciones Siruela, 1994.

Cirujano Marín, Paloma, Teresa Elgorriaga Planés, and Juan Sisinio Pérez Garzón. *Historiografía y nacionalismo: 1834–1868.* Madrid: Centro de Estudios Históricos, C.S.I.C., 1985.

de Man, Paul. *Blindness and Insight: Essays in the Rhetoric of Contemporary*

Criticism, 2d edition. Minneapolis: University of Minnesota Press, 1983.

———. *The Rhetoric of Romanticism*. New York: Columbia University Press, 1984.

———. *Critical Writings, 1953–1978*. Edited by Lindsay Waters. Minneapolis: University of Minnesota Press, 1989.

Díaz, José Pedro. *Gustavo Adolfo Bécquer: Vida y obra*, 3d. edition. Madrid: Gredos, 1971.

Elorza, Antonio. *La modernización política en España (Ensayos de historia del pensamiento político)*. Madrid: Ediciones Endymion, 1990.

Ensayos literarios y críticos por D. Alberto Lista y Aragón. Edited by José Joaquín de Mora. Seville, 1844.

Espronceda, José de. *El Estudiante de Salamanca / El diablo mundo*. Edited by Robert Marrast. Madrid: Castalia, 1982.

Flitter, Derek. *Spanish Romantic Literary Theory and Criticism*. Cambridge: Cambridge University Press, 1992.

Fynsk, Christopher. *Heidegger: Thought and Historicity*. Ithaca, N.Y.: Cornell University Press, 1986.

García Berrio, Antonio. *Teoría de la literatura (La construcción del significado poético)*, 2d edition. Madrid: Cátedra, 1994.

Hölderlin, Friedrich. *Essays and Letters*. Translated by Thomas Pfau. Albany: State University of New York Press, 1988.

Jover Zamora, J. M. *La civilización española a mediados del siglo XIX*. Madrid: Espasa-Calpe, 1992.

Juaristi, Jon. *El linaje de Aitor: La invención de la tradición vasca*. Madrid: Taurus, 1987.

Juretschke, Hans. *Vida, obra y pensamiento de Alberto Lista*. Madrid: C.S.I.C., 1951.

———. *Origen doctrinal y génesis del romanticismo español*. Madrid: Ateneo, 1954.

King, Edmund L. "What is Spanish Romanticism?" *Studies in Romanticism* 2 (Autumn 1962): 1–11.

Kirkpatrick, Susan. *Las Románticas: Women Writers and Subjectivity in Spain, 1835–50*. Berkeley: University of California Press, 1989.

Lacoue-Labarthe, Philippe. *La Poésie comme Expérience*. Paris: Christian Bourgois Editeur, 1986.

Lacoue-Labarthe, Philippe, and Jean-Luc Nancy. *L'absolu littéraire: Théorie de la littérature allemand*. Paris: Editions du Seuil, 1979.

Llorens, Vicente. *Liberales y románticos: Una emigración española en Inglaterra*. Mexico City: El Colegio de México, 1954.

López Garrido, Diego. *La Guardia Civil y los orígenes del estado centralista*. Barcelona: Editorial Crítica, 1982.

Marichal, Carlos. *La revolución liberal y los primeros partidos políticos en España, 1834–1844*. Madrid: Ediciones Cátedra, 1980.

Marrast, Robert. *José de Espronceda y su tiempo*. Translated by Laura Roca. Barcelona: Editorial Crítica, 1989.

Menéndez Pidal, Ramón. *Los españoles en la historia*. Edited by Diego Catalán. Madrid: Espasa-Calpe, 1987.

Moreno Alonso, Manuel. *Historiografía romántica española: Introducción al estudio de la historia en el siglo XIX*. Seville: Universidad de Sevilla, 1979.

Nemoianu, Virgil. *The Taming of Romanticism: European Literature and the Age of Biedermeier*. Cambridge: Harvard University Press, 1984.

Pageard, Robert. *Bécquer: leyenda y realidad*. Edited by Hans Juretschke. Madrid: Espasa-Calpe, 1990.

Peers, E. Allison. *A History of the Romantic Movement in Spain*. 2 vols. New York: Cambridge University Press, 1940.

Romero Tobar, Leonardo. *Panorama crítico del romanticismo español*. Madrid: Castalia, 1994.

Santí, Enrico Mario. "Sor Juana, Octavio Paz and the Poetics of Restitution," *IJHL* 1, no.2 (1993): 101–129.

Sebold, Russell P., ed. *Gustavo Adolfo Bécquer*. Madrid: Taurus, 1982.

Shaw, Donald L. "The Anti-Romantic Reaction in Spain," *Modern Language Review* 63 (1968): 606–611.

Silver, Philip W. *Nacionalismos y Transición: Euskadi, Catalunya, España*. San Sebastián: Editorial Txertoa, 1988.

———. *Luis Cernuda: el poeta en su leyenda*. Madrid: Alfaguara, 1972. Reprint, Madrid: Castalia, 1995.

Vicens Vives, Jaime. "El romanticismo en la historia." In *El romanticismo*. Edited by David T. Gies, 155–173. Madrid: Taurus Ediciones, 1989.

Warminski, Andrzej. "Monstrous History: Heidegger Reading Hölderlin." *Yale French Studies* 77 (1990): 193–209.

Williams, Anne. *Art of Darkness: A Poetics of Gothic*. Chicago: University of Chicago Press, 1995.

INDEX

Abrams, M. H., 6, 7; *Natural Supernaturalism*, 55–56, 113; romantic plot, 6, 55–56, 71, 100, 113; on Wordsworth, 56

Addison, Joseph: *The Pleasures of the Imagination*, 22, 48, 84, 157n.19; personification in, 84

Alborg, Juan Luis: *Historia de la literatura española* IV, 67; on Spanish romanticism, 67–69

ancien régime, 8, 9, 14, 138n.22

antiromanticism, 4, 136n.2, 137n.14

authoritarian liberalism (Elorza), 3, 14, 15, 30, 39. *See also* liberalism (Spanish)

Aullón de Haro, Pedro, 4

Azorín: "The Genius of Castile," 31, 34–35; "Life and Death," 35, 145n.94

Ballbé, Manuel, 39

Basque nationalism, 32–33, 36–37, 144n.91, 146nn.102, 103

Bécquer, Gustavo Adolfo, ix, xiii, 54, 70, 71, 72; on Augusto Ferrán, 92, 93–95; and Blair, 82, 86, 94; blockage in, 85, 95; and *cante jondo*, 90, 92–93, 94–97, 159n.44; *Cartas desde mi celda*, 54, 80–81, 89; *Cartas literarias a una mujer*, 48, 78, 79, 95; and Cernuda, 43, 72, 79; and Chateaubriand, 54, 74, 75, 88, 90; and critical history, 75–76; descriptive hypotyposis in, 82, 85–86, 91, 97, 158n.31; and figures of passion, 83, 86, 90; and figures of reason and expression, 83, 90; and Herrera, 80; *Historia de los templos de España*, 52, 54; historicality in, 54, 66; imagination in, 77–78, 96; ineffable in, 89–90; and Kantian sublime, 85; and Lista, 86; and modern Spanish poetry, 54; and modernity, 74–75; on Murillo, 89–90; as national-romantic, 76, 91, 92; national-romantic sublime in, 73, 80; personification and sublime in, 82–83, 86–87, 91, 159n.40; and picturesque, 80; and preromanticism, 98; resolute repetition in, 155–156n.11; *Rimas*, 90–97; "San Juan de los Reyes," 75, 79, 84–88; on statues, 79, 88; sublime and beautiful in, 88, 89; traditionalism of, 54, 92, 97; and Wordsworth, 83

Benítez, Rubén: on Bécquer, 73–76, 77–79

Benjamin, Walter: on romanticism, 43–44

Biedermeier romanticism, 6–7, 11, 70. *See also* romanticism

Blair, Hugh: on imagination, 17; *Lectures on Rhetoric and Belles Lettres*, 6, 17, 82

Böhl de Faber, Juan Nicolás, 4, 5, 7, 12, 18; Cecilia (daughter), 52

Bosch Gimpera, Pere, 30–31, 36

bourgeois revolution, xiii, 8, 9, 11, 25, 33; and romantic historians, 25, 27, 29, 30

Burke, Edmund: and Bécquer, 94; and Cernuda, 119, 121

RUIN AND RESTITUTION

was composed electronically
using Goudy types, with displays in
Optima, Ovidius, and Type Embellishments One.
The book was printed on 60# Natural Hi Bulk acid-free,
recycled paper, Smyth sewn, and cased into Pearl Linen cloth
over 80-point binder's boards, with head bands and matching
end leaves, by Braun-Brumfield, Inc.
The dust jackets were printed by Vanderbilt University
Printing Services. Jacket Design is by Tom Ventress;
book design and composition are by Bard Young.
Published by Vanderbilt University Press
Nashville, Tennessee 37235